WHY IS IT SO HARD

Becoming a PEOPLE PERSON In The Post COVID-19 Era

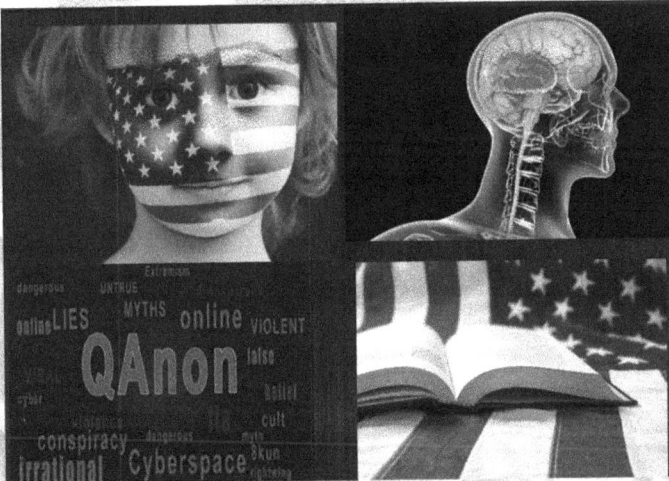

Ervin (Earl) Cobb
Charlotte D. Grant-Cobb, PhD

OTHER BOOKS BY
Ervin (Earl) Cobb and Charlotte D. Grant-Cobb, PhD

Living a More Thoughtful Life
Thinkable Thoughts and Relevant Reflections

Situations and Leadership
Short Stories and Lifelong Lessons

Leadership Front and Center
A Decade of Thought and Tutelage

The SMART Leader and the Skinny Principles
How to Win and Lead within Any Organization

Driving Ultimate Project Performance
Transforming from Project Manager to Project Leader

**The Official Leadership Checklist and Diary
for Project Management Professionals**

The Leadership Advantage
Do More. Lead More. Earn More.

God's Goodness & Our Mindfulness
Responding versus Reacting to Life Changing Circumstances

Focused Leadership
What You Can Do Today To Become a More Effective Leader

Transition
Solace and Comfort for the Broken Hearted

Pillow Talk Consciousness
Intimate Reflections on America's 100 Most Interesting
Thoughts and Suspicions

Navigating the Life Enrichment Model™

Living a Richer Life
Getting the Most out of Life's Gifts and Circumstances

Until I Change
Affirmations for Mastering Personal Change

Ervin (Earl) Cobb and Charlotte D. Grant-Cobb, PhD
PRAISE FOR THEIR WORK

"There is nothing better than a good story. Utilizing very relevant stories that you can easily identify with tied to the highly actionable Skinny Principles makes for a great formula. A very useful and timely book for all professionals looking to advance their leadership skills."

— Barbara Cooper, CIO Toyota North America – Retired

"Charlotte and Earl are leaders and can teach leadership, a rare combination. The Smart Leader should hold a prominent place in your professional library."

— Jim Grigsby, President/CEO Jim Grigsby Consulting

"Master Teachers is my description of these authors. The Smart Leader is a must read for all leaders; especially for generations of future leaders."
— Selma C. Dean, ED.D. , Pastoral and Community Counselor, Educator, Inspirational Speaker

"Written from practical experience and success. An inspiration!"

— Robert Bunnett, Chief Operating Officer, LSI

"Earl Cobb has done it again with his new book. Earl is that rarest of authors. He writes with the power of someone who has been there."

— Doug Russell, Marketing Director, SmartPro Financial

"Mr. Cobb has captured the pure essence of Leadership in this work. His broad-based experience guides his insight in every topical area."

— Albert L. McHenry, Ph.D., Emeritus Faculty, Arizona State University

"Busy leaders need practical guidance and an easy-to-follow format which is what this book provides. The authors have culled their years of experience and in a story format. By doing so, they have provided a path for leaders to follow. I hope others may benefit from their expertise and apply the "Skinny" Principles to their respective paths. Kudos!"

— Dr. G. Mick Smith, Executive Regional Director, Challenger School Foundation

Ervin (Earl) Cobb and Charlotte D. Grant-Cobb, PhD
PRAISE FOR THEIR WORK

"As major transitions in the world are transpiring, leadership requires a broader and deeper understanding of today's organizations and the individuals that lead them. The SMART Leader and the "Skinny" Principles proffers that leaders are expected to act and think differently, not just to survive, but to thrive in this changing organizational landscape."

— Rufus Glasper, Ph.D., President and CEO, League for Innovation, Chancellor Emeritus, Maricopa Community Colleges

"Mr. Cobb has been meticulously working on advancing what is known in the realm of Leadership Development. He is a proven author of several books, a well-known speaker, a leader, and has a genius approach to leadership development. The information that he provides in his latest body of work is "textbook worthy" and I highly recommend all colleges/universities/companies adopt this body of work to teach Leadership Development."

— Jonathan Hebert, M. Eng, PMP, Ph.D., Program

"The Cobbs have written a leadership book that is easy to read with practical, apply it right now, techniques. This book is chock full of tips, techniques, and best practices in leadership that will be of value to new leaders of any generation. Their "Skinny" Principles, shared in each chapter, will undoubtedly be earmarked and highlighted by readers and referred to regularly. This book is a MUST READ for new leaders. Plus, leaders who have been in their role for a while will likely also find a nugget or two to take away and apply."

— Gina Abudi, MBA, President, Abudi Consulting Group, LLC, Author of *Implementing Positive Organizational Change: A Strategic Project Management Approach*, J Ross Publishing, 2017

DEDICATION

We dedicate this book to you, the reader. If you are so moved after reading this book, please share the book and its messages with others. This includes family, friends, neighbors and those who you would like to better understand as human beings. It just might start an insightful, constructive and civil conversation. A conversation which could bring out the best in *yourself* as a human being. It may also help you began to respect the uniqueness of others who have had different experiences as an American.

Published by RICHER Press
An Imprint of Richer Life, LLC
5710 Ogeechee Road, Suite 200-175, Savannah, Georgia 31405
www.richerlifellc.com

Cover Design: RICHER Media USA
Photograph: Bigstock

Volume book discounts are available for groups, companies and organizations. Contact the publisher for information and order instructions.

Library of Congress Control Number: 2021945860

Why Is It So Hard
Becoming A People Person in the Post-COVID-19 Era

Ervin (Earl) Cobb and Charlotte D. Grant-Cobb, PhD

1. Psychology & Counseling   2. Politics & Social Sciences
3. Self-Help/Self-Management

(pbk : alk. Paper)

ISBN: 978-1-7335693-4-7 Paperback
ISBN: 978-1-7335693-7-8 Hardback

PRINTED IN THE UNITED STATES OF AMERICA

CONTENTS

PREFACE

When we returned to our home in Phoenix on December 24, 2019, we were eager to spend the holiday season with our daughter and three grandchildren.

We had planned to stay in Phoenix for a few months to get things in order after dumping dozens of boxes in our garage after selling our Tucson home in July.

The boxes had gone untouched because we spent most of the last five months of 2019 at a new second home we purchased in Savannah, Georgia in August. Based on what was needed to be done at the Phoenix home, we made our American Airlines flight reservations to return to Savannah on April 1, 2020.

Christmas at home with the family was a blast. The month of January was quite productive. We managed to sort through the boxes and clean out most of the other "stuff" which had accumulated in the garage over the ten years we had lived there.

By mid-February we were feeling good about being able to check-off all the things on our "to-do" list and get back to

Savannah as planned. We were excited about finally spending some quality time with our new Georgia neighbors and to participate, for the first time, in an annual Mardi Gras celebration to be held down on the riverfront in historic Savannah in mid-April.

Starting back in January, like most Americans, we had been following the news regarding the sudden emergence of a SARS-like illness causing a form of viral pneumonia in China.

Watching the news stories, we tracked the spread of the virus from China into Europe. Then, around mid-February, we learned that the CDC confirmed an infection in California that would represent the first individual in the U.S. to become infected with the virus despite not visiting a foreign country or encountering an infected person. This was not good news. We quickly began to sense that this could be serious and became genuinely concerned.

After the President declared in mid-March the coronavirus pandemic to be a national emergency in the U.S., and the Arizona Governor joined other State Governors in issuing "stay-at-home" orders, we had to quickly decide on where we wanted to be during this major health crisis — in Phoenix or in Savannah.

We made the decision to return to Savannah on the first of April as planned while we still had an option to get out of Arizona. However, because of the unknown nature of this mysterious virus, we did not want to use the return airline tickets we had already purchased.

Since we had some household goods requiring to be moved to the Savannah house, we decided to rent a small U-Haul trailer and drive the 2,200 miles back to Savannah. It would be the same drive we made in August 2019, during the initial phase of our move into the Savannah home.

So, we once again planned a four-day road trip with three overnight stops at roadside hotels in El Paso, Texas, Grand Prairie, Texas and Meridian, Mississippi.

Even though we would only stop for gas and prepared evening meals in the hotel rooms, it was not a bad trip — until we left Grand Prairie heading to Meridian.

After stopping for gas, we began to enter an on-ramp to Interstate 20 when we had to make a sudden stop. The U-Haul trailer somehow flipped to one side and slammed into the back of our new Hyundai Santa Fe. The damage was much more serious that we initially thought. As we pulled onto the Interstate, we heard the muffler dragging on the roadway. I immediately pulled off the road and got out of the car to inspect the situation.

Fortunately, I was able to find a spare "bungee cord" and tied the muffler up to eliminate the dragging. However, I knew we would not get too far with this quick fix. While I focused on driving as carefully as I could in the right lanes at moderate speeds, Charlotte searched and found a Hyundai dealership about 30 miles away in Jackson, Mississippi. Around 2:30 in the afternoon we arrived at the auto dealership safely. We were welcomed by Jim, the service advisor on duty.

As he and his technicians were evaluating the damage to the car, Charlotte and I were thinking through where we could stay in Jackson for the evening. We assumed the dealership would have to order parts and could not repair the exhaust system damage anytime soon.

When we left Texas earlier that morning, we felt that we were successfully in the home stretch of a long trip. It was a trip taken during an unprecedented time in recent American history. Now, suddenly, we were not sure how this day or week would end.

When Jim and his team asked me to come into the garage to look at the damage while the car was still up on the lift, I was thinking the worst — either it could not be fixed today or it would cost us much more than normal because they had us in a bind.

First, they showed me the "bungee cord" they had removed from the muffler. It was almost burned in half. It was obvious that my "quick fix" might have lasted for only another couple of miles.

Then, they showed me the damage the trailer had done to the exhaust system. However, one of the technicians had devised a method to secure the "bent" muffler. He also used a thick metal bracket to make sure that everything would stay in place for the rest of our trip.

This was good news. I thanked them for taking the time to rigorously evaluate the damage and for coming up with a way to quickly secure the muffler. This would allow us to get to our Meridian, Mississippi stop before dark. With a smile, I asked Jim to finalize the paperwork — knowing that we were prepared to pay them fully for their responsiveness and quick thinking.

Once they brought our car back out of the garage and helped to re-attach the trailer, Jim looked at me and said, *"Mr. Cobb, I hope you and Mrs. Cobb get home safely…and…there is no charge"*.

Being totally surprised, we thanked Jim and his team again. We drove away and safely arrived at our hotel that evening. After we arrived in Savannah late the next day, we had a chance to relax and reflect upon the long trip. We both observed how different this trip was compared to our drive across country in August 2019.

Of course, with the onset of the COVID-19 pandemic, we had developed a new routine of wiping everything down with sanitizers, staying away from other people as much as possible and controlling our internal "self-talk". We have found that the conscious act of controlling *self-talk*, helps manage, the anxiety caused by new levels of uncertainty, in our life.

Nonetheless, relative to the muffler incident, we could not keep our minds from wondering, *What if the incident with the trailer had happened near another town in Mississippi?* or *What if the incident had happened later in the evening when auto dealerships would be closed?* or *What if we had found ourselves the victims of an apathetic, unsympathetic, racist or opportunistic person?* A person who perhaps might not be interested in helping us or just eager to take advantage of us and the moment — instead of someone like Jim.

As time moved on and with the help of cool, morning walks along the beaches of Hilton Head Island, we soon stopped wondering about the incident. We were thankful to be home, to have each other and to be safe from the dreadful disease — a disease that we did not realize at the time would eventually claim over 600,000 American lives — the most of any single country in the world, as of the writing of this book.

What continues to be a constant in our minds even to this day is the memory of Jim and his kindness. During our unplanned stop in Mississippi, Jim's actions were those of what we would call, being a genuine, *people person*. It was not that we had not moved beyond the 2,200-mile road trip back to Savannah. It was just the realization that there appears to be so few people like Jim in American society these days.

Late in the summer of 2020 and into the Spring of 2021, we began working on refining and processing our thoughts regarding the *people person* metaphor, that we had intuitively coined.

After months of thought, we finally settled on the following characterization of a *"people person"*.

> "A *people person* is an individual who acts daily upon the belief that the pinnacle of human life is not anchored in misinformation, egotism, tribalism, hatred, jealousy or selfishness, but in one striving to bring out the best in oneself, as a human being and respecting the uniqueness and the humanity of others."

In this context, we began to become increasingly curious as well as intellectually challenged by these two questions.

1. *Why is it so hard and what will it take to become a people person in today's ultra-partisan, politics-driven and socially divisive American culture?* and

2. *Will the primary factors inhibiting most Americans from becoming people persons present a greater challenge in a post-COVID-19 era?*

To this day, we continue to think that finding useful answers to these questions is extremely important if there is any chance of moving toward national unity and becoming a more civil and humanitarian society.

We believe that finding useful answers to these questions will require someone to untangle, and examine the complexities, and interrelatedness of four fundamental aspects of American life:

- The search for societal unity within America.
- The role of humanity within daily life.
- America's struggle with diversity and its past; and
- The invasiveness of societal influences.

Thus, the genesis of this book.

INTRODUCTION

Why Take This Journey

A s we began to lay the foundation for this project, we wanted to make sure that this book would continue our goal of using our literary work to express and re-enforce our lifelong mantra of *shaping thoughts and changing lives for the better.*

For the over forty years we have been together as a couple, we have had many new and varied life experiences. We have worked for many companies, have had many job titles, have lived in many places and have enjoyed the enlightenment of many people from many walks of life.

Consequently, some of our most interesting life experiences and stories have found beneficial ways to be incorporated within our work.

In this regard, we decided to use as the preface of this book a real-life story which created the origin of what you have just read. This story was written as an article immediately after completing our 2,200-mile cross-country road trip during the onset of the COVID-19 pandemic. We believe it does a great job in painting a picture of the emotional landscape surrounding the book's thesis as well as shedding some light on our mental state at the time.

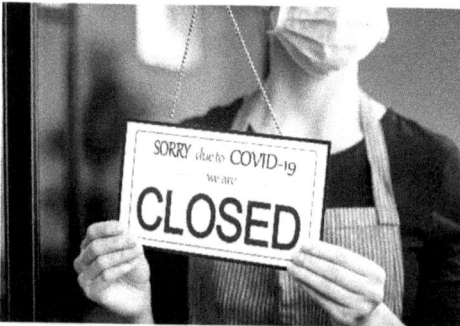

The last eleven months of 2020 were unprecedented times. It was a period in history that was shared by hundreds of millions of people in every segment of American society.

All non-essential businesses were being shut down. Stay-at-home and shelter-in-place orders were being issued across the country. Schools were abruptly closed and Americans were becoming infected with the virus and dying horrible deaths by the tens of thousands.

Like most other Americans, for months on end, we were isolated in our home, only leaving the house to get groceries. We watched closely as a nation of unexpecting people struggled to come to grips with the unique fear of a global pandemic being caused by a deadly, and uncontrollable disease.

After a few months of watching the news stories, we could not dismiss and had to seriously question the undeniable display of selfishness, hatred, political polarization and healthcare disparities within American society — even during a national crisis.

Based on social and economic status, the degree of hardship and the number of infections and deaths varied significantly from community to community.

From the hoarding of sanitizers and paper products to the inflation of prices for household necessities, to weaponizing the act of wearing a face cover or mask, the glaring lack of national cohesiveness during this global crisis overshadowed the *societal unity* that was being requested and expressed by many Americans.

At the same time, and in contrast, as we reflected upon the auto incident back in April 2020, we were reminded of Jim, the *people person*, who, with one small act of kindness, made us feel a real sense of *community* during crisis. A human feeling that allowed us to experience, in an unexpected place, the gift of kindness by which *people persons* can identify with and provide one another.

It was this insightful and troubling comparison that ignited our inquisitiveness to investigate the societal influences within American society today, which feeds an anti-humanitarian culture.

These social influences are omnipresent and, individually and at times, in combination, present psychological barriers, which prevent many thoughtful people from becoming true *people persons*.

Our recognition and concern with the growing invasiveness and impenetrability of these barriers, which were so apparent during the 2020 presidential election cycle and throughout the coronavirus pandemic, were the catalysts that moved us to take the journey we have documented within the pages of this book.

The Essence and The Mission

the purpose / 'pɜːpəs / th...
purpose /'pɜːpəs/
the reason for doing so...
the purpose of your visi...
...purpose ...e because...

"The purpose of human life is to serve, and to show compassion and the will to help others." —**Albert Schweitzer**

As we have grown and developed as persons and as human beings for more decades than we care to remember, our belief has become stronger in the spirit of the message conveyed in the above quote attributed to Albert Schweitzer, an Alsatian-German philosopher, musicologist, medical missionary and a 1953 Noble Prize awardee.

As Aristotle once argued, *"Happiness is the ultimate goal of human existence because it is the only thing we do only for itself. People want to be wealthy, famous, and powerful only because these things, they believe, will lead them to happiness".*

As devoted writers and published authors for over two decades, our belief has also become stronger in the need for all good literary work of this type to possess and express its purpose. This allows the reader to suitably participate in, and truly benefit from the exchange of sincere thought.

In this respect, the two questions presented in the preface of this book succinctly encompass our purpose and sets forth the *essence* and the *mission* of this literary journey.

The First Question

THE |ESSENCE

Why is it so hard and what will it take to become a people person in today's ultra-partisan, politics-driven and socially divisive American culture?

This question is the *essence* of our journey and formulates the target of the discussion in Chapter One, titled, *Why Is It So Hard: Unity, Humanity, People* and *Influence.*

In Chapter One and throughout this book, we explore *why it is so hard* for many of us to become a *people person.*

We do this by using a presentation approach we developed to communicate and illuminate *conscious-centric* thought. This approach quietly integrates revealing, photographic images and the most important literary work of others into the main discussion.

For this book, we have found this approach to be an effective method to help connect *"thought with feelings,"* while untangling, and examining the complexities and the interrelatedness of four Fundamental Aspects of American life.

These Fundamental Aspects are:

1. The search for societal unity within America.

2. The role of humanity within daily life.

3. America's struggle with diversity and its past; and

4. The invasiveness of societal influences.

Furthermore, we introduce what we believe to be a primary set of what we call, *Framing Factors*, which support and greatly contribute to the obstacles associated with becoming a *people person,* in America today.

Based upon recent national surveys, these obstacles have furthered what appears to be a growing anti-humanitarian, and anti-democratic faction among Americans. The increase in social and political divide was apparent, in a series of incidents over the past few years.

At the top of the list were three incidents:

- The rising volume of divisive rhetoric, hate-baiting, and anti-democratic actions occurring across the country and within the highest levels of state, and federal government. This reverberation seemed to have peaked during the 2020 presidential election.

- The confrontational episodes of terror and belligerence during the COVID-19 pandemic — all in defiance of federal and state orders associated with business closures, community gatherings and the wearing of protective face covers and masks; and

Dareh Gregorian, Yahoo News, June 15, 2021

- The shocking January 6, 2021, insurrection at the United States capital where the 117th Congress was meeting to count the results of the Electoral College vote and certify the winner of the 2020 presidential election.

By all accounts it was a historic rebellion, led by an overwhelmingly white, conservative and angry group of President Trump followers. The entire day-long episode was televised and broadcasted for the world to see. Sadly, the uprising ended in deaths and destruction.

According to several national news investigations and reports, the brazened forthrightness and organized violence of the January 6th uprising, deeply disturbed most Americans from all political spectrums.

The *framing factors* we present and discuss in this book are prevalent throughout the American social, and political landscape today. We believe that a deeper examination of the *rationale and impacts* of each of these factors, and their influence on various aspects of America's social, economic, and political constructs can shed considerable light on the answer to the question — *Why is it so hard to become a true people person in America?*

The Second Question

THE | MISSION

Will the primary factors inhibiting most Americans from becoming people persons present a greater challenge in a post-COVID-19 era?

This question soundly sets forth our *mission* to identify and characterize the social, economic, and political influence of each of the factors. In doing so, we closely examine the rationale, and impacts. In our research, we found that the anti-humanitarian effects of several of these *framing factors* were amplified during the COVID-19 pandemic, continues at this elevated level today.

We include throughout the discussion of each factor, relevant thoughts from the literary work of other contemporary authors, scholars, historians, and social activists who have documented, and publicly shared insights regarding obvious cultural, and personal challenges associated with America becoming a kindlier, and humanitarian society.

We conclude the discussion of each factor by outlining some commonsense approaches that can be used as a *starting point* for anyone interested in taking on the challenge of becoming more of a *people person.*

Within the dissertation, we make no attempts to persuade anyone that one set of thoughts, conclusions and beliefs are the only valid perspectives on the topic. We simply set forth what we believe to be a candid, honest and contemporary discussion.

To this point, we have included at the end of the book, note pages for you to use to record and *ponder* your own thoughts, conclusions and perspectives, on the thirteen primary topics we will discuss. You may want to record your thoughts, as you attentively read, and absorb each chapter.

If you are so moved after reading this book, please share the book, its messages and your own thoughts with others. This includes family, friends, neighbors and those who you would like to better understand as human beings. It just might start an insightful, constructive and civil conversation. A conversation which could bring out the best in *yourself* as a human being. It may also help you began to respect the uniqueness of others who have had different experiences, as an American.

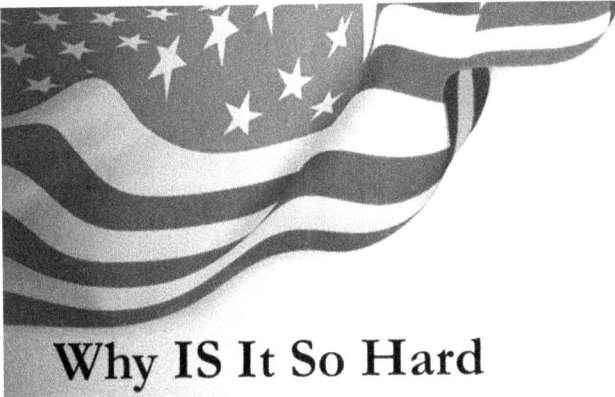

Why **IS** It So Hard

CHAPTER ONE

Why Is It So Hard: Unity, Humanity, People and Influence

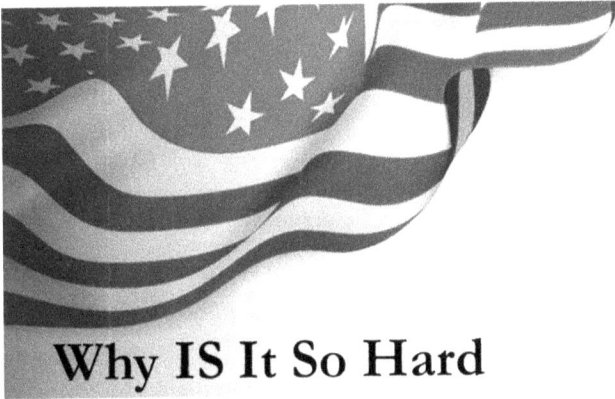

Why **IS** It So Hard

Why Is It So Hard: Unity, Humanity, People and Influence

Police officer seen on video kneeling on the neck of George Floyd.
Photo: Contributed to AP News

"After a few months of watching the news stories, we could not dismiss and had to seriously question the undeniable display of selfishness, hatred, political polarization and healthcare disparities within American society. It was clearly revealed for all to see."

There were many national events that stood out during the peak of the COVID-19 pandemic in America. However, none was as emotionally moving and dramatizing as the video footage of how George Floyd met his horrific death under the knee of a Minneapolis police officer, named Derek Chauvin, on Memorial Day 2020.

According to Dr. Malik Simba, California State University, Fresno, History and Africana Studies professor, and the author of *Black Marxism and American Constitutionalism: An Interpretive History from Colonial Background to the Great Depression* :

"Floyd's murder almost immediately generated protests that continued in some cities into September 2020. By conservative estimates, these protests have

involved more than 26 million Americans in 2,000 cities and towns in every state in the United States, making these the most widespread protests around one issue in the history of the nation."

In a May 2020 article by Jelani Cobb, a professor at Columbia University's Graduate School of Journalism and contributor to The New York Times on race, politics, history and culture wrote:

"The video of Floyd's death is horrific but not surprising; terrible but not unusual, depicting a kind of incident that is periodically reenacted in the United States. It's both necessary and, at this point, pedestrian to observe that policing in this country is mediated by race."

Professors Simba and Cobb's comments regarding the death of George Floyd are not only from the prospective of their academic and professional studies, but also from their heritage, and American experience.

Even as scores of millions of Americans in 2,000 cities were protesting what appeared to be such a horrible, and inhumane incident, occurring right before their eyes, there were hundreds of millions of other Americans who chose not to protest. Perhaps many of these Americans were not in the position to protest, or did not view the need to protest, but were just as disturbed about the apparent brutal nature of the incident.

However, being aware of the huge national divide on the issue of social justice and human rights in this country, we must also consider that many Americans, who viewed the same video, were moved to object to the protests, and to any change in their perspective on policing in America.

Despite the well-documented and historically tragic outcomes that unscrupulous policing has had on the lives of racial and ethnic minorities for centuries, these Americans may have had different life experiences with policing, and many may believe that this news story was being blown out of proportion.

This viewpoint and its apparent absence of humanity may be concerning to many others. But, in America we all have the right to our own opinions and perspectives.

As we mentioned in the Introduction, in this book we do not attempt to persuade anyone that one set of thoughts, conclusions and beliefs are the only valid perspectives on this topic.

Nevertheless, there were thousands of photographs taken during the pandemic documenting a shocking level of selfishness, hatred, political polarization and healthcare disparities within American society. We selected this photograph because we believe that this one, clearly illuminates the lack of kindness and humanity that exist in many facets of American life today.

If you look closer at the photograph below of George Floyd being subjected to a needless and horrific death you can not only see but can almost feel the cold-heartedness and inhumane action taken by one "person" against another "person".

Photo: Contributed to AP News

When we look at the action that this photograph captures, we see and feel the antithesis of any action that would be expected from a *people person*.

It is important to understand and factor into the discussions, you are about to read, our characterization of a *people person*, which is: *"A people person is an individual who acts daily upon the belief that the pinnacle of human life is not anchored in misinformation, egotism, tribalism, hatred, jealousy or selfishness, but in one striving to bring out the best in oneself as a human being and valuing the uniqueness and the humanity of others."*

Our characterization embodies an *approach* to living one's life. It is an approach which recognizes and commits to what it means to be the *human* within the sphere of humanity. This approach prioritizes mutual respect and the well-being of other humans — even where there is conflict or disagreement.

We believe that Americans, as a people, essentially agree with this characterization. Many might even intellectually believe that they are living the life of a *people person* and, for some, this would be true. Then, why is it so hard for most Americans to truly become a *people person*?

In the following four sections of this chapter, we present what we believe is a thoughtful dissertation, based on our years of relevant experience and recent research as well as the literary work of other authors, scholars, historians, news correspondents, bloggers and social activists.

We believe that this type of candid and carefully constructed presentation can provide some credible insights and possible answers to those with an open mind. However, parts of the discussions may perhaps introduce new, unaddressed questions regarding *the burden* that we all must bear —*the burden of existing as a "human being", and the undeniable need to both protect ourselves, _and_ live with others, in a mutually productive manner, for the long-term survival, of our democracy.*

The Search for Societal Unity Within America

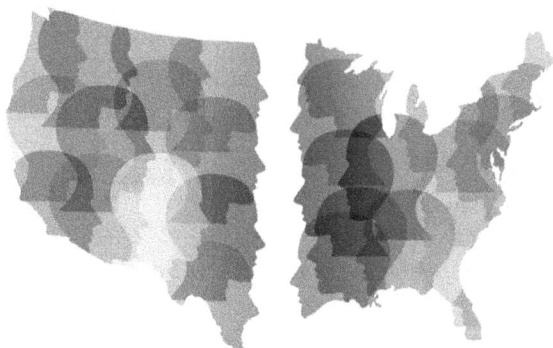

"Unity is a little like exercise: A great idea, a noble idea, but hard, and all too easy to forego. Yet history tells us that America works best when just enough of us see politics as a mediation of differences rather than as total, unrelenting warfare. It is not a partisan point to observe that a change in administrations offers the country an opportunity to assess anew the purpose and possibilities of our public life."

—TIME Magazine article written by Samar Ali, Bill Haslam and Jon Meacham, February 8, 2021

As most of us learned in grade school, at the beginning of the preamble to the U.S. Constitution we find the words, *"We the people"*. The fact that the U.S. Constitution begins with those three words should give all Americans comfort. Just think. Even though the search for *societal unity* within America may seem an impossible task, just knowing that unlike many other societies, our country has ideals and principles which have effectively fueled aspirations such as *unity* for over two centuries.

An August 2020 survey conducted by the Associated Press, revealed the following:

"There is something 93% of American voters can agree upon — they believe it is important for our leaders to focus on things that bring people together. That total includes 71% who say it's very important. Ninety-six percent (96%) of Democrats believe it's important to focus on bringing people together. So do 92% of Republicans and 90% of independent voters."

During our research and studies of America's search for *societal unity*, we were not surprised by the Associated Press findings that a governing majority of Americans seek more national unity.

America's rich, rebellious, rumbustious and sometimes acrimonious history is peppered with calls for local, state and federal leaders to *bring people together*.

Perhaps a serious analysis of the lessons learned from America's history, could be very instrumental in empowering the majority of Americans today, to come to an agreement and resolve one of America's most crucial and civic dilemmas. A dilemma, which must be tackled to obtain a sustainable degree of *societal unity* within the nation. We describe the dilemma as follows:

"Within a 240-year-old Federation of 50 states, which has morphed into a diverse, culturally polarized and economically asymmetric population of over 300 million people, how can we obtain the widely accepted compromise necessary to protect its two-party, representative government? — a novel experiment in governing that has been at the core of American-style democracy since our nation's founding."

With that in mind, we were somewhat surprised to learn from recent surveys that although a governing majority of Americans seek more national unity, most Americans lack a functioning knowledge of factual American history. They also do not value how our thinly veiled democracy has survived and how it works. Here are some of survey finding which support this observation.

- A 2014 National Assessment of Educational Progress report found that only 18 percent of 8th graders were proficient or above in U.S. History, and only 23 percent in Civics.

- A 2008 study by the Intercollegiate Studies Institute surveyed more than 2,500 Americans and found that only half of adults in the country could name the three branches of government.

- Ironically, many of those who are politically active admit that they formed their strongest opinions on what's right and what's wrong with America, from listening to AM talk radio, watching cable news and participating in social media.

- As a result, many Americans struggle with identifying and verifying the truth from falsehoods. A 2018 Pew Research Report indicates the following:

Nearly two-thirds of adults find it hard to tell what's true when elected officials speak

% of U.S. adults who say it is ____ to tell the difference between what's true and what's not true when ...

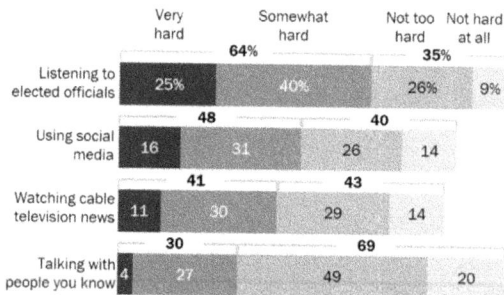

	Very hard	Somewhat hard	Not too hard	Not hard at all
		64%		35%
Listening to elected officials	25%	40%	26%	9%
		48	40	
Using social media	16	31	26	14
		41	43	
Watching cable television news	11	30	29	14
		30	69	
Talking with people you know	4	27	49	20

Note: Those who did not give an answer are not shown.
Source: Survey conducted Nov. 27-Dec. 10, 2018.
"Trust and Distrust in America"

PEW RESEARCH CENTER

These are independent, intriguing and insightful observations. However, more importantly, the observations reveal an extremely important reality — *Americans do not believe in the same set of facts.* This reality heightens the challenge of obtaining *societal unity.*

As we all know, having or believing the facts, is an undeniable prerequisite for achieving the goal of *"bringing people together"*. We believe that this is a major *disconnect* contributing to *why it is so hard,* for the average American to gain honest momentum toward valuing humanity and becoming a *"people person"*.

As we untangled and looked beneath the fabric of American history, we were enthralled by the degree to which the polarization, divisiveness, disagreement and anger among *"We the people"* have overshadowed the aspiration for societal unity for most of our nation's history.

Within the Constitution of the United States, *"We the people"* describes a society that holds in common a commitment to *equality*, *liberty*, and *dignity*. The U. S. Constitution, while sighted daily in federal courts as the defender of certain individual rights — *such as, the right to own firearms with no restrictions, and the right to defy the Center of Disease Control orders designed to protect public health during a global pandemic* — turned 240 years old on September 17, 2021.

The study of the U. S. Constitution and America's factual history reveals that after searching for more than two centuries for *societal unity*, there have been only 68 out of the past 221 years where Americans have lived in a country where "unity" prevailed — and even then not all Americans experienced the feelings of *equality*, *liberty*, and *dignity* as set forth in the Constitution.

Therefore, by all informed accounts, the aspiration of *"bringing people together"* or "uniting" has historically been more the *exception* than the *rule*. Consequently, it is not surprising that in the 21st century political world, when partisans say they want "unity", what they really want is for their opponents to agree with them.

Thomas Jefferson Building, the oldest structure in the Library of Congress complex.
Image from the Library of Congress, Washington, D.C.; photography by Carol M. Highsmith (digital file no. LC-DIG-highsm-03196)

According to the many documents in the United States Library of Congress, there have been three periods in American history where "unity" has prevailed. During these periods, Americans have experienced economic growth by *agreeing to invest* in national infrastructure, the education of the American people, and in initiatives which moved more Americans into the mainstream of experiencing the *equality*, *liberty*, and *dignity* as set forth in the U. S. Constitution.

At the end of this Section, we have included a brief overview of the three periods in American history where "unity" prevailed, as ascertained from the Library of Congress. We have also included some relevant excerpts from an article titled, *Unity: A Principle That Could Save America* posted on the website of the National Center for Constitutional Studies in June 2020. We think that both literary works are worthy of reading and deep reflection.

We believe that a thorough reading of these works, along with others sighted in the references listed at the end of the book, could possibly reveal some surprising unknowns. They also might reflect some light upon the questionable origins of how *"We the people"* were able to gain and maintain national unity during these periods in America's history.

The historical unknowns may include a deeper understanding of the following:

- How the demand for labor during World War II caused millions of Americans to move to the Atlantic, Pacific and Gulf coasts, and why, by the end of the war, the moves had improved America's economy when compared to other countries in the world; and

- How the 1929 stock market crash, which abruptly ended the widespread prosperity of the 1920s, turned out to be an unsuspecting *double-edged sword* — causing the *great economic depression* as well as setting the political stage, and creating the broad public cooperation needed to generate a period in American history which created much of the current physical and social infrastructure we utilize, benefit from, and enjoy today.

Our research has led us to believe that, because of the complex relationship that exist between *democracy*, *individualism*, *capitalism* and *human rights*, the formation of any successful effort to unify America again, for another extended period, must include a robust, and national reflection upon America's *true* history — and the need for *"We the people"* to accept the reality that, we cannot escape *humanity* and *compromise*, if America expects to become, as President Ronald Reagan once called, *"… A shining city upon a hill, whose beacon light guides freedom-loving people everywhere".*

Periods of American Unity Since 1900
Source: United States Library of Congress

1. The Post War United States, 1945-1968

The entry of the United States into World War II caused vast changes in virtually every aspect of American life. Millions of men and women entered military service and saw parts of the world they would likely never have seen otherwise. The labor demands of war industries caused millions more Americans to move largely to the Atlantic, Pacific, and Gulf coasts where most defense plants were located. When World War II ended, the United States was in better economic condition than any other countries in the world. Even the 300,000 combat deaths suffered by Americans, paled in comparison to any other major belligerent.

2. Great Depression and World War II, 1929-1945

The widespread prosperity of the 1920s ended abruptly with the stock market crash in October 1929, and the great economic depression that followed. The depression threatened people's jobs, savings, and even their homes and farms. At the depths of the depression, over one-quarter of the American workforce was out of work. For many Americans, these were hard times. The New Deal, as the first two terms of Franklin Delano Roosevelt's presidency were called, became a time of hope and optimism. Although the economic depression continued throughout the New Deal era, the darkest hours of despair seemed to have passed. In part, this was the result of FDR himself. In his first inaugural address, FDR asserted his *"firm belief that the only thing we have to fear is fear itself."* As FDR provided leadership, most Americans placed great confidence in him.

3. Progressive Era to New Era, 1900-1929

The early 20th century was an era of business expansion and progressive reform in the United States. The progressives, as they called themselves, worked to make American society a better and safer place in which to live. They tried to make big business more responsible through regulations of various kinds. They worked to clean up corrupt city governments, to improve working conditions in factories, and to better living conditions for those who lived in slum areas. A large number of whom, were recent immigrants from Southern and Eastern Europe. Many progressives were also concerned with the environment and conservation of resources.

From - *Unity: A Principle That Could Save America*, **June 2020**
National Center for Constitutional Studies (NCCS)

"Era of Good Feelings" Leads to National Unity 1814-1824

For nearly a decade after the War of 1812, America experienced some remarkable, unifying events. President James Monroe declared in his first inaugural address that "local jealousies are rapidly yielding to more generous, enlarged, and enlightened views of national policy." The strife between political parties disappeared and the parties themselves became nearly nonexistent.

The unity was so pervasive that when Monroe ran for reelection in 1820, he won every electoral vote but one. It is said that one elector cast a vote against him simply because the elector believed only Washington should enjoy the honor of a unanimous election.

During Monroe's second term, the people were so united in their vision for America that President Monroe was able to take the bold step to declare to the world that the Western Hemisphere was off limits to any further colonization by European powers.

He also promised that the United States would leave European affairs to the countries of Europe. This was a bold position for a small, new country to announce, but this announcement by President Monroe, later known as the Monroe Doctrine, became the cornerstone of American foreign policy for many years.

Sectionalism and Secession leads to Civil War 1855-1866

By this time in our nation's development, good feelings had disappeared. Political, social, and economic differences were dividing the nation.

Even though a compromise now and then kept a lid on the boiling factions, issues such as slavery, state nullification of federal laws, and tariffs kept raising their ugly heads to a point where compromise was no longer possible. Some states began to think getting completely out of the Union was the answer, and so, they passed resolutions of secession.

The eventual result, of course, was the most destructive and divisive period of war this country had ever experienced. It was a war on our own soil--citizen against citizen, brother against brother, neighbor against neighbor.

History calls it the Civil War. Paul Harvey more correctly names it the "Uncivil War". Whatever one calls it, the happenings of this period should sound a warning to Americans about the dangers of factions and talk of disunion.

The Role of Humanity Within Daily Life

"Humanity means caring for and helping others whenever and wherever possible. Humanity means helping others at times when they need that help the most, humanity means forgetting our selfish interests at times when others need our help. Humanity means extending unconditional love to every living being on Earth."

— Anju Chhatwani, an early childhood educator and Early Years Foundation Stage (EYFS) professional.

A round 500 BC, the Chinese teacher, philosopher and political theorist Confucius once said, *"Without knowing the force of words, it is impossible to know more"*.

As we all know, words have power. How we understand and internalize the meaning of words create opinions that influences our beliefs, determines our behavior, and ultimately establishes how we see ourselves, how we see others and how we see our world. The power of words is derived from our emotional responses when we read, speak or hear them.

How old were you when you first heard the word *humanity?* More importantly, how old were you when you first began to appreciate the essential role that humanity can play in our daily lives.

Unfortunately, when we hear the word *humanity* used in our daily life in America, it is mostly linked with negative connotations.

With the growing hostility and factions in the United States, and around the world, we more often think of humanity in terms of human rights violations, activities we would consider inhumane and organizations seeking donations by tugging on our emotions in late night infomercials.

While on the contrary, the word "humanity" embraces what's most positive within us as being human beings. We believe one of the most comprehensive meanings of the word *humanity* that we have found is as follows:

"Humanity is a collection of positive traits that humans should have in them. These traits or qualities include kindness, compassion, honesty, courage, tolerance towards differences, empathy, respect, integrity, thoughtfulness, etc."

Of course, not every human has all these qualities and in the same proportion. However, we believe that everyone has some of these qualities. Many scholars believe that *"these qualities are what makes us human."*

We interpret the significance of this belief as follows:

- When positive human qualities are practiced regularly, it transforms a "man" or "woman" into a "human"; and

- The lack of these qualities often makes a man or woman appear wicked or inhumane and may lead to the demise of humanitarian norms and humane societies.

In our research we have found that many economic, political, and social issues being faced in many aspects of daily life in America are grounded in the *"lack of humanity"*.

The Lack of Humanity

As we mentioned in the Introduction of this book, our experiences during the height of the COVID-19 pandemic in 2020 left us questioning the tangible level of humanity in America today.

"After a few months of watching the news stories, we could not dismiss and had to seriously question the undeniable display of selfishness, hatred, political polarization and healthcare disparities within American society — even during a national crisis."

In 2020 and now in 2021, the United States, as well as the world, were facing exceptionally challenging situations caused by the onset of the coronavirus pandemic. The rapid spread of the disease traumatized the world. The systems in place to address and deal with the inequalities and the casualties of a deadly global pandemic were grossly inadequate. The healthcare, educational and economic systems within most countries collapsed during the pandemic. We believe that many of the reasons for these situations occurring can be linked to a global lack of humanity.

One of the major reasons is that many countries spend more on military and weapons, than the public health and education sectors. Additionally, the speed of the global spread, and the huge death toll can be tracked to the fact that many people, of all persuasions, refused to believe in the legitimacy of the coronavirus during the early stages of the pandemic. As a result, instead of the most advanced societies in the world bringing unified efforts to fight the pandemic, it was the battles between governments, political parties, and a divided populous that prevented the *force of humanity* from assisting in the minimization of deaths, and the loss of livelihoods.

We believe that the rise of Anti-Asian violence, acts of social injustice and partisan politics in all regions of the United States during the global crisis, reflect the lack of humanity, within American society.

The Role of Humanity

Earlier in this discussion, you will recall that our characterization of being a *people person* embodied an *approach* to living one's life. The act of *striving to bring out the best in oneself as a human being and valuing the uniqueness and the humanity of others,* not only creates the opportunity to allow others to experience kindness and civility, but also contributes to the collective release of the force of humanity.

In our research, we have learned and come to believe that, in the purest sense, humanity, and humanitarian cultures have transformative forces which can lay the foundation for, resolving issues within societies that wealth, political power, selfishness, celebrity, threats, coercion, regulations, laws, punishment or physical destruction have failed to do, since human existence.

Here are four significant issues we believe that humanity and humanitarian cultures could resolve and why.

- **The Uniting of Humans Across the Globe**

As we know, humans from different parts of the world pursue various religions and cultures. This means they follow different rituals and have different cultural values. These differences can create a gap among humans in different parts of the world. However, the language of humanity is one force that can unite humans despite their differences. We believe that *human connection* is an energy exchange between people who care for one another. It has the force to deepen the moment, inspire change and build trust.

- **The Creation of a Lasting Peace**

One of the qualities of humanity is to be tolerant towards those who share different opinions and backgrounds. When we tolerate the differences, there is less chaos in the world, and less chaos implies the lack of destruction and establishment of peace. We believe that if all humans and governments use the *weapon of humanity*, there will be more peace and happiness in the world.

- ### The Increase in Ethical Behavior

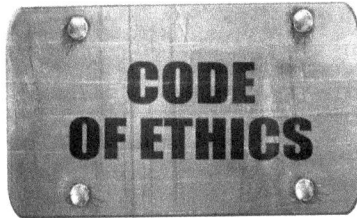

As hard as it is to agree on *the facts*, these days in America, it is a fact that humanity embraces moral values of ethical behavior. Many institutions and organizations develop an ethical code of conduct for their team members. These codes are based on the fundamental traits of humanity. If each of us, as a human, work on developing our own *collection of positive traits* there would not be the need to forcefully demand ethical behavior from everyone. We believe that humanity can eliminate many issues of moral values and ethics from society.

- ### The Reduction in the Crime Rate

We believe the increase in the number of crimes in the United States and in the world today is mainly due to the lack of humanity. There are times when law abiding people are forced to crimes because of social and economic predicaments. However, the root cause remains the lack of humanity from people in power who are busy with self-preservation and ignore the needs of the most impoverished, and the most less-educated segments of the society.

If there is widespread humanity, there would most likely be a reduced crime rate.

When viewed from this perspective, the role of humanity within daily life reveals itself as a very practical and positive one.

By visualizing a world where humans are globally united, where peace prevails, where everyone behaves ethically and where crime is almost non-existent, most of us can see the intrinsic value in humanity and recognize why the battle of becoming a *people person* is one that is worthy of fighting.

However, within an American society, which is struggling with diversity and its past, and whose national politics has unconsciously moved in a direction that embraces viewing political opponents as enemies and choosing voters through partisan gerrymandering versus resolving factual differences, it becomes extremely difficult for the *force of humanity* to prevail.

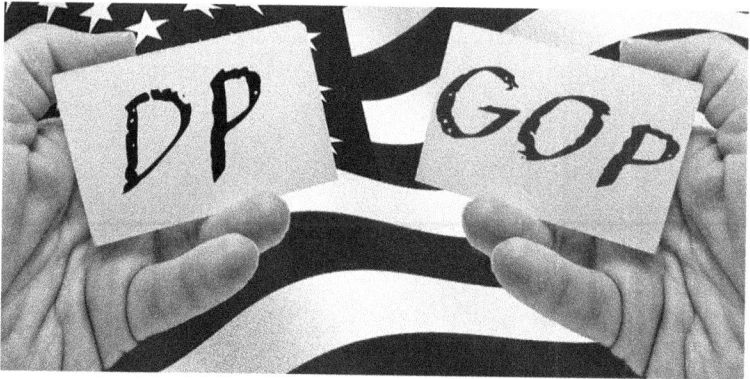

We discuss, examine and attempt to untangle many of these issues and other societal matters that contribute to the growing challenge of becoming a *people person,* in the next two sections of this chapter and the remaining chapters.

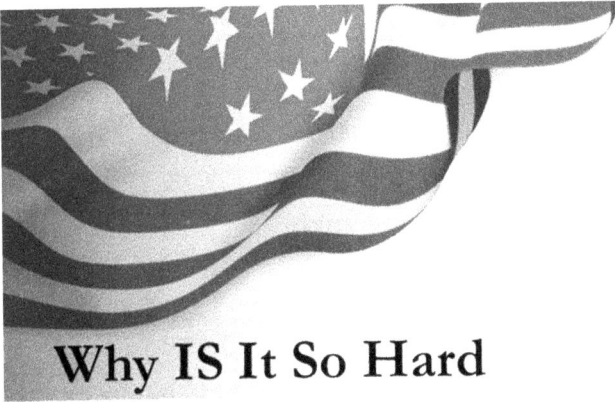

Why **IS** It So Hard

America's Struggle With Diversity and Its Past

"Diversity means a mixture of different things. It means people of all kinds from different backgrounds, of different ages, and with different beliefs. But Americans often use the word 'diversity' to mean people of different races."

—USAHello.org, June 11, 2021

(Evan Vucci/AP)

"The White House's Office of Management and Budget notified agency heads on Sept. 4th that federal workplaces will no longer be allowed to conduct 'divisive, anti-American propaganda' training that focuses on race theory and white privilege."

— Jessie Bur, Federaltimes.com, September 8, 2020

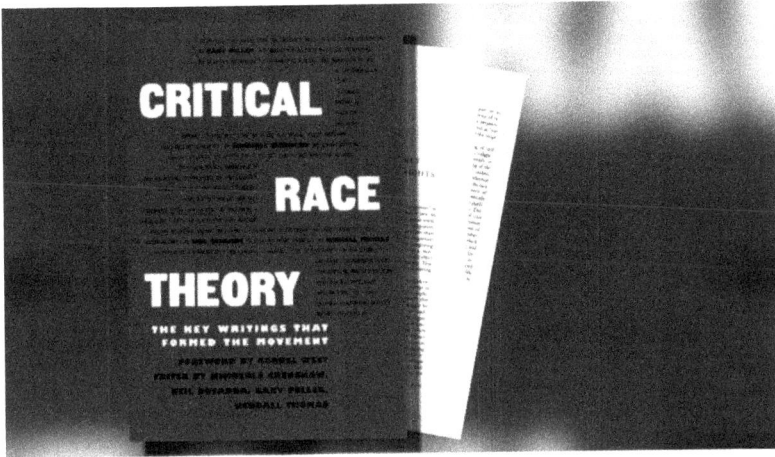

WINK Digital Media, 2021

"It's [Critical Race Theory] *a concept that's been around for decades and that seeks to understand and address inequality and racism in the US. The term also has become politicized and been attacked by its critics as a Marxist ideology that's a threat to the American way of life."*
——**Faith Karimi, CNN, May 10, 2021**

"CRT [Critical Race Theory] *is not a diversity and inclusion "training" but a practice of interrogating the role of race and racism in society that emerged in the legal academy and spread to other fields of scholarship.* [Kimberle Williams] *Crenshaw—who coined the term "CRT"—notes that CRT is not a noun, but a verb. It cannot be confined to a static and narrow definition but is considered to be an evolving and malleable practice. It critiques how the social construction of race and institutionalized racism perpetuate a racial caste system that relegates people of color to the bottom tiers. CRT also recognizes that race intersects with other identities, including sexuality, gender identity, and others. CRT recognizes that racism is not a bygone relic of the past. Instead, it acknowledges that the legacy of slavery, segregation, and the imposition of second-class citizenship on Black Americans and other people of color continue to permeate the social fabric of this nation."*

——**From "A Lesson on Critical Race Theory" written by Janel George, American Bar Association, January 12, 2021**

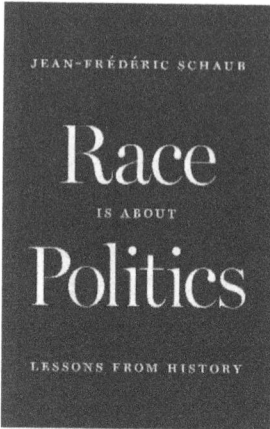

JEAN-FRÉDÉRIC SCHAUB

Race

IS ABOUT

Politics

LESSONS FROM HISTORY

Amazon.com

"Racial divisions have returned to the forefront of politics in the United States and European societies, making it more important than ever to understand race and racism… we need to rethink the widespread assumption that racism is essentially a modern form of discrimination based on skin color and other visible differences. On the contrary, to understand racism we must look at historical episodes of collective discrimination where there was no visible difference between people. Built around notions of identity and otherness, race is above all a political tool that must be understood in the context of its historical origins."

—Race Is about Politics: Lessons from History, Jean-Frédéric Schaub, Princeton University Press, January 8, 2019

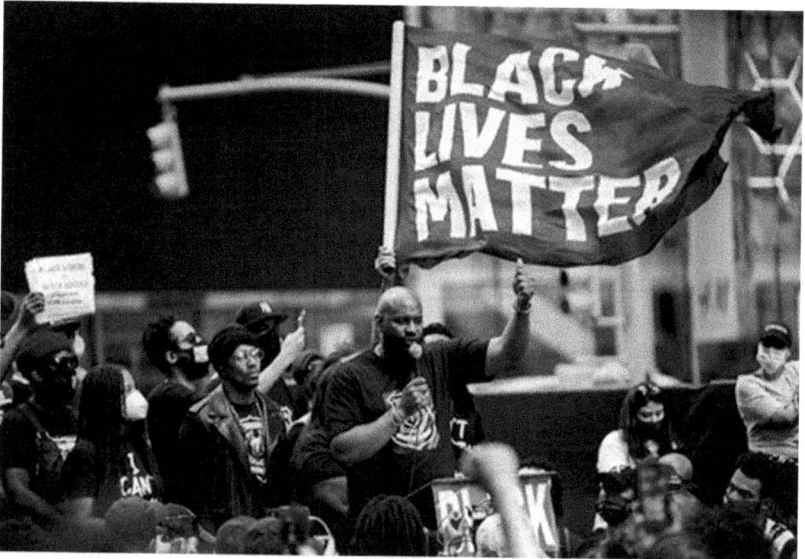

—Black Lives Matter protest, Times Square, New York City, June 7, 2020
Photo by Anthony Quintano (CC BY 2.0)

Majorities of whites, blacks and Hispanics say racial and ethnic diversity is very good for the country

% saying it is ____ for the country that the U.S. population is made up of people of many different races and ethnicities

	Very good	Somewhat good	Net
All adults	57	20	76
White	55	20	75
Black	59	16	75
Hispanic	60	20	80
Rep/Lean Rep	39	26	65
Dem/Lean Dem	71	14	85
Among whites			
HS or less	41	22	63
Some college	55	21	77
Bachelor's+	69	18	87
Among blacks			
HS or less	44	18	63
Some college	65	19	84
Bachelor's+	80	7	87

Note: Figures may not add to subtotals due to rounding. Whites and blacks include those who report being only one race and are non-Hispanic. Hispanics are of any race. This question was asked of a random half of the sample; estimates for Asians are included in the total but are not shown separately due to small sample size.
Source: Survey of U.S. adults conducted Jan. 22-Feb. 5, 2019.
"Americans See Advantages and Challenges in Country's Growing Racial and Ethnic Diversity"

——Pew Research Center May 8, 2019

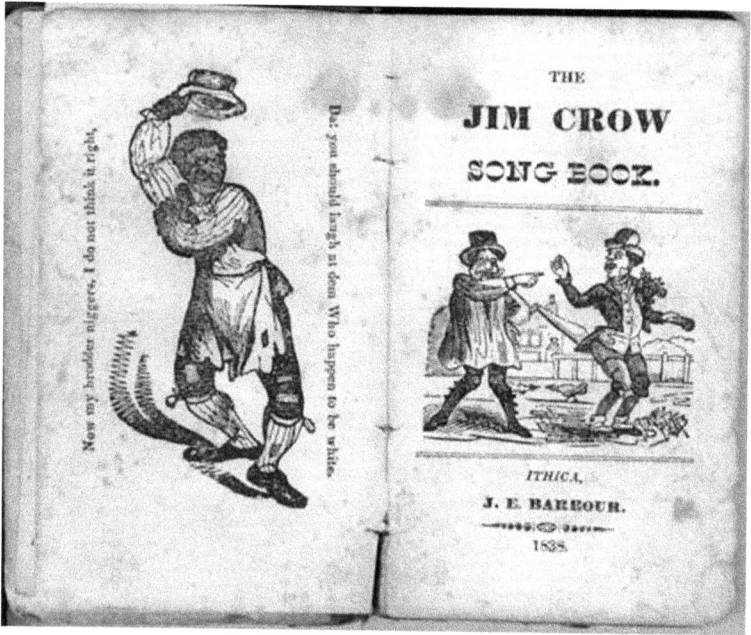

—**National Museum of American History**

aving been born as African Americans in the 1950s and during the Jim Crow era in the southern United States, we are no strangers to the prominent role that race and race relations has played, and continues to play within many aspects in the lives of scores of millions of Americans.

Three steps forward and one step backwards would be a quick "snapshot" shared by most minorities and marginalized Americans who are unwillingly mired in this demoralizing social and political game.

In contrast, we have had the opportunity to work hard, earn advanced degrees, work closely alongside, and befriend Caucasian Americans of varying persuasions, with most being within Fortune 100 companies. So, we also are no strangers to understanding how this broad cross section of these Americans see and cope with race and race relations in their lives.

A quick "snapshot" in this regard would perhaps range from, *embracing to deploring racial barriers,* to *unknowingly supporting the racial divide hidden in racial politics and the fear associated with change.*

Having successfully "straddled" both sides of this issue, and now having the opportunity to think deeply about the struggles within American society to extinguish the divisiveness of racial inequality, and discrimination, we think the graphic and sobering messages presented at the beginning of this section does a good job in characterizing what we have found in our research. To be brief in presentation, and comprehensive in sharing our findings, we have thoughtfully condensed what we believe are the three primary barriers, preventing America, as a nation, from moving toward becoming a more humanitarian society as it pertains to *"race, gender, ethnicity, class, and discrimination".*

Our research indicates that, to honestly think about and fully understand what is required to move beyond the prolonged status quo, is a major step toward, taking the actions necessary, to remove these barriers. Here are the three things we believe are required.

1. We, *as a people,* must arrive at a point where a reliable majority of Americans understand that *"Diversity means a mixture of different things"* that are independent of race and gender. Only by arriving at this point will the cohesiveness, energy, determination and resources necessary to expand America's global competitiveness and provide quality of life for all its citizens. From this point, we as a nation will be able to value and strategically utilize the full cadre of distinctive skills, cultural differences, life experiences, socio-economic backgrounds, and language proficiencies available.

2. We, *as a people,* must arrive at a point where a reliable majority of Americans openly reject racial politics and transform our political systems to enable them to be truly representative of the people. We must strive to support and elect political officials, who are truly *"people persons"* and

believe in the words of a phrase that can be traced back over 2,600 years to 6th Century B.C., *"United we stand, divided we fall"*. Of course, the tenacity of a unified public will be required to, realistically overcome the entrenched barriers of gerrymandered congressional districts and polarized political parties; and

3. We, *as a people,* must arrive at a point where a reliable majority of Americans create a path, short of another civil war, to help a deep-seated plurality of Americans to understand, and buy into the value of accepting, teaching and learning from all of America's rich history, instead of attempting to "re-write" it. From this point, we as a nation can free-up a tremendous amount of kindness, human resources, ingenuity, trust and productivity that has been burdened by selfishness, prejudice, apathy, discrimination and institutionalized racism for centuries.

While reading Jean-Frédéric Schaub's book, *Race Is about Politics: Lessons from History*, during our research for this topic, the insight that continues to resonate in our minds is this passage: *"To understand racism, we must look at historical episodes of collective discrimination where there was no visible difference between people"*. In the book, Schaub reminds us that, *"A key turning point in the political history of race in the West occurred not with the Atlantic slave trade, and American slavery, as many historians have argued, but much earlier, in fifteenth-century Spain and Portugal, with the racialization of Christians of Jewish and Muslim origin. These Christians were discriminated against under the new idea that they had negative social, and moral traits that were passed from generation to generation through blood, semen, or milk. An idea whose legacy has persisted through the age of empires to today."*

We believe that all Americans must come to grips with the fact that since the existence of early *humans*, one of the major challenges to humanitarianism has been the attraction of power, selfishness, discrimination, and "otherness".

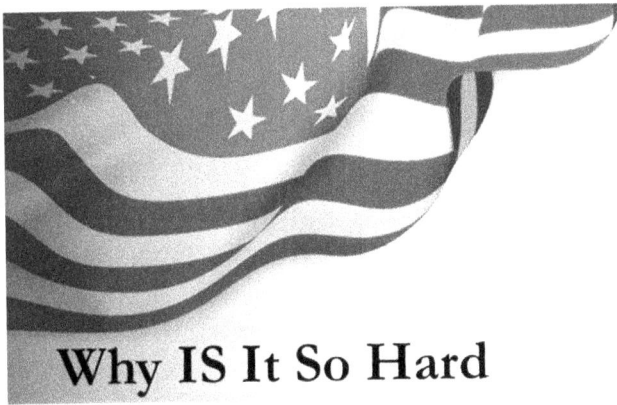

Why **IS** It So Hard

The Invasiveness of Societal Influences

During our research, we found that to adequately discuss the *invasiveness* of societal influence, we must first step back, and present a short overview of the vast amount of study that has been done on the *nature of society*.

We will then discuss our findings regarding the societal influences, and how they *unconsciously* invade our minds and erect challenging mental barriers to becoming a true *people person*. You might be surprised to learn that this is a natural invasion which goes on in silence. A continuous invasion which directly affects our strongest opinions, beliefs, and how we react and respond to daily circumstances.

The Nature of Society

The term society is derived from the Latin word *'Socius'* which means a companion, association or fellowship. The American society that we all are a part of consists of the mutual interaction of us as individuals, as well as the structure of our relationships.

Consequently, when we refer to the American society in this discussion, we are referring not to a group of people but to the complex pattern of *rules of interaction*, that arise among them. The mere gathering of Americans does not constitute the American society. The American society refers to the complicated network of social relationships by which each American is interrelated with other Americans. Therefore, the American society is abstract, and not tangible in nature. We cannot touch it but we can feel it. In other words, the American society resides in the minds of individual Americans.

The question of the *nature of society* is intimately connected to the relationship of *man* and *society*. There are mainly two theories of the relationship between *man* and *society*: the *Social Contract Theory* and the *Organic Theory.*

- The Social Contract Theory states that: *"People live together in society in accordance with an agreement that establishes moral and political rules of behavior. Some people believe that if we live according to a social contract, we can live morally by our own choice and not because a divine being requires it".*

- The Organic Theory states that: *"Political entities continually seek nourishment in the form of gaining territories to survive in the same way that a living organism seeks nourishment from food to survive."*

The three main points that we would like to highlight here as it relates to the *invasiveness* of societal influences are:

- ✓ The discussions and debate of the *nature of society* dates to the days of Socrates, Plato and Aristotle. Such intense philosophical focus and concern underscore the important role that societies and societal influences can play in either the supporting or rejecting of humanitarian qualities such as *kindness, compassion, honesty, etc.*

- ✓ The history of mankind has documented that a functional and humanitarian society must, *"live together…in accordance with an agreement that establishes moral and political rules of behavior";* and

- ✓ Yes. It is a natural phenomenon that has been known to mankind for thousands of years: *"Political entities continually seek nourishment in the form of gaining territories* [from others in society] *to survive".*

The Invasiveness of Societal Influences

EXERCISE: Take a few minutes to review the photographs below and the news headlines which follow. Then, write down *what you see* and *how you feel* about these images and the headlines.

Neo-Nazis and White Supremacists March through the University of
Virginia Campus in Charlottesville, Virginia, on August 11, 2017.
Getty/Samuel Corum/Anadolu Agency

COVID-19 Anti-Lockdown Protests in the United States
By Becker1999 from Grove City, OH - cIMG_0355, CC BY 2.0, April 2020

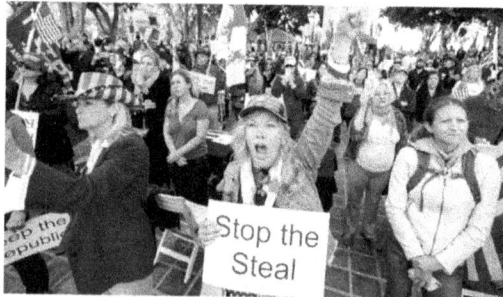

Supporters of US President Donald Trump protest in
Los Angeles, California, on January 6, 2021
By Ringo Chiu | AFP | Getty Images

Major News Headlines in the U.S. Media
August 11, 2017 - July 5, 2021

—Armed Protesters Demonstrate Against Covid-19 Lockdown at Michigan Capitol

By Lois Beckett, The Guardian News & Media Limited, April 2020

— Heavily Armed Protesters Gather Again At Michigan Capitol To Decry Stay-At-Home Order:

By Abricail Censky, NPR, May 14, 2020

—US Protests Could Bring Coronavirus Surge

By VOA News, May 31, 2020

—How White Supremacy Returned to Mainstream Politics

By Simon Clark, July 1, 2020

—Politics is Wrecking America's Pandemic Response

By Jonathan Rothwell and Christos Makridis, The Brookings Institution, September 17, 2020

—How This Year's Antiracism Protests Differ from Past Social Justice Movements

By Amna Nawaz and Saher Khanovements, PBS News Hour, Oct 28, 2020

— Trump Supporters Protest at Statehouses Across The U.S. as Capitol Hill Demonstrations Turn Violent

By Leslie Josephs, CNBC, January 6, 2021

—FAA Says Airlines Have Reported about 2,500 Incidents of Unruly Passengers - Majority of the incidents have had to do with mask wearing

By Alison Fox, Travel & Leisure Co, May 25, 2021

—It's Out of Control. Airlines, Flight Attendants Want Stiffer Penalties for Unruly Passengers

By Leslie Josephs, CNBC, June 22, 2021

—Steady Term of the Supreme Court Ends with Politically Fraught Cases that Reveal Divisions

John Fritze, USA TODAY, July 5, 2021

What the images and headlines you have just reviewed reveals is only a snapshot of a significant portion of the contemporary abstract of American society between August 11, 2017, through July 5, 2021.

As we stated earlier, the American society is not any one group of people but the complex pattern of *rules of interaction,* that arise among society members. By critically viewing each image, from your perspective, for the social value or harm being portrayed; and evaluating each headline for what you believe it contributes or removes from the fragile mosaic of America's diverse culture, you accomplished a patriotic duty that not many Americans do very often.

What did you do? You took the time to deeply think about, internalize, and assess the realities surrounding some of the social networks, which are the embodiment of the images and headlines you have just reviewed.

Many social networks in America today typically use these events and behaviors to publicly express the beliefs, attitudes and passions of its members. They are established and maintained by various social, political and religious factions within American society. Their members have opinions that have been galvanized into a group mindset by cable television, talk radio, and social media. A mindset which has been strengthen by what is perceived by them as acceptable *rules of interaction.* Most members of distinctive social networks, but not all, are citizens, expressing concerns about their safety, their family traditions and their perceived superiority within American society. They feel more comfortable being a part of a social group when expressing their opinions and beliefs outside of the home. Some, at times, find themselves taking unruly and careless actions without regard of the possible irreversible effects their actions may have on public health, other's security or the preservation of America as a democratic republic.

The notes you have written down, assuming you did take part in the "Exercise" as requested, are as close as you can get to touching the society we all share. As we also mentioned earlier, due to its construct, societies cannot be *touched*. However, we can *feel* the complicated network of social relationships and the results of the overt actions. Many of the feelings come in the form of fear, depression, disappointment, resentment, rage and a loss of hope and trust.

As a reminder, in America's democracy, all of the perceptions and concerns you noted after reviewing the photographs and headlines, are consistent with America's *rules of interaction*. Social rules that are condoned and accepted by the *governing* majority, which is elected by us, the American people.

We believe that most of the Americans taking part in such overt events and activities reflected in the images, and headlines you have just viewed, and read, have two things in common.

- First, they are worthy Americans consciously aware of the overt actions they take, and are obviously passionate, and emotionally connected to the ideas they believe and convey.

- Secondly, most of them honestly, and sincerely arrived at the belief that their overt social, and political behaviors are acceptable within the current *rules of interaction*.

Our research indicates that many Behavioral Psychologist believe that *"most human behavior is learned in interaction with our environment, and that all behaviors are learned through experience."*

The Role of Societal Influence

Now, let's examine the role that *societal influences* play is our daily lives and how their *invasiveness* unconsciously erects mental barriers to a *people person's* focus on *"striving to bring out the best in oneself as a human being and respecting the uniqueness and the humanity of others."*

EXERCISE: Take a few minutes to thoughtfully read the research summaries on this and the following page about *Societal Influence* and *The Unconscious Mind*. This exercise can help you grasp and appreciate our discussion of the *invasiveness* of societal influences. It may also be beneficial as we examine the *rationale* and *impacts* of what we consider to be the primary set of social influences within the American culture today in the subsequent nine chapters.

Societal Influence

> Research has identified a few common requirements that contribute to the recognition of a group: interdependence, social interaction, perception as a group, commonality of purpose, and favoritism.

> There are both positive and negative implications of group influence on individual behavior. This influence is useful in the context of work and team settings; however, it was also evident in Nazi Germany.

> Groupthink is a psychological phenomenon that occurs within a group of people, in which the desire for harmony or conformity in the group results in an incorrect or deviant decision-making outcome.

> Groupshift is the phenomenon in which the initial positions of individual members of a group are exaggerated toward a more extreme position.

> Deindividuation is a concept in social psychology that is generally thought of as the losing of self-awareness in groups. Theories of deindividuation propose that it is a psychological state of decreased self-evaluation and decreased evaluation apprehension that causes abnormal collective behavior.

— Lumen Learning. Introduction to Psychology, State University of New York OER Services

The Unconscious Mind

McLeod, S. A. (2015). *Unconscious mind*. Simply Psychology.

"While we are fully aware of what is going on in the conscious mind, we have no idea of what information is stored in the unconscious mind.

The unconscious contains all sorts of significant and disturbing material which we need to keep out of awareness because they are too threatening to acknowledge fully.

The unconscious mind acts as a repository, a 'cauldron' of primitive wishes and impulse kept at bay and mediated by the preconscious area. For example, Freud (1915) found that some events and desires were often too frightening or painful for his patients to acknowledge, and believed such information was locked away in the unconscious mind. This can happen through the process of repression.

The unconscious mind contains our biologically based instincts (eros and thanatos) for the primitive urges for sex and aggression (Freud, 1915). Freud argued that our primitive urges often do not reach consciousness because they are unacceptable to our rational, conscious selves.

People use a range of defense mechanisms (such as repression) to avoid knowing what their unconscious motives and feelings are.

Freud (1915) emphasized the importance of the unconscious mind, and a primary assumption of Freudian theory is that the unconscious mind governs behavior to a greater degree than people suspect. Indeed, the goal of psychoanalysis is to reveal the use of such defense mechanisms and thus make the unconscious conscious.

Freud believed that the influences of the unconscious reveal themselves in a variety of ways, including dreams, and in slips of the tongue, now popularly known as 'Freudian slips'. Freud (1920) gave an example of such a slip when a British Member of Parliament referred to a colleague with whom he was irritated as 'the honorable member from Hell' instead of from Hull."

Cultural Influences Within America

As we started this journey, we initially were puzzled as to why we as *human beings* find it difficult to embrace *humanity* in all aspects of our lives when it seems intuitively that this should be a *natural*.

However, as we mentioned in our discussion of the *nature of society* and as you were reminded when you read the two research summaries on the previous two pages, we as human beings are also *naturally susceptible* to environmental influences.

Regardless of possible skepticism by some, we think that most Americans would agree that social psychologists have documented over centuries, overwhelming evidence regarding how the *human mind* works. Believe it or not, none of us can escape the mind's natural process of doing most of our thinking for us, in silence.

Understanding this explains why, embracing *humanity* within a social culture that *does not* wholeheartedly embrace the practice of humane behavior within societal *rules of interaction*, will always be a challenge. With this accepted and understood, what intrigued us as we continued our research was not the nature of *societal influence* but its degree of *invasiveness* within the construct of the American society in the 21st century.

In medicine the word *invasiveness* is defined *as "the ability of microorganisms to enter the body and spread in the tissues."*

In the context of this discussion, we define the word *invasiveness* as, *"the ability of talk radio, cable news, social media, political parties, trade lobbyists, think tanks, religious groups and even manufacturers of drugs and medicines to enter our subconscious mind to spread their preferences, beliefs, and desires in the tissues of American culture".*

It was this thought-provoking and troubling comparison that initially ignited our inquisitiveness to investigate and untangle the societal influences within American society today, which feeds an anti-humanitarian culture.

As we said earlier, these social influences are omnipresent, and individually, and at times, in combination, present psychological barriers, which prevent many thoughtful people from becoming *people persons*.

The following pages offer some insights and examples which reveal a portion of the *ecosystem* and the *magnitude* of the *invasiveness* of organized societal influence within our country. We believe that the *invasions* have intensified and have become more sophisticated as we have *advanced* technologically, intellectually and politically as Americans and as human beings.

Most of the invasions are not malicious, misguiding or what you would consider undemocratic. However, all the individuals, groups, organizations, companies and institutions responsible for developing and financing the multitude of daily invasions, wish to *influence* our society to accept their preferred social philosophy, attitudes and politics. The strategic influence of governmental decisions and laws is key to establishing their preferences within America's social *rules of interaction*.

Lobbying and Political Influence

"The primary goal of much of the money that flows through U.S. politics is this: Influence. Corporations and industry groups, labor unions, single-issue organizations - together, they spend billions of dollars each year to gain access to decision-makers in government, all in an attempt to influence their thinking." — **opensecrets.org**

In the chart below, data from opensecrets.org is used to break down lobbying efforts. It combines all political contributions and lobbying spending from January 1998 to March 31, 2020. These figures are calculations by the Center for Responsive Politics based on data from the Senate Office of Public Records.

Pharmaceuticals/Health Products	$4,450,373,773
Insurance	$2,973,247,470
Electric Utilities	$2,567,713,347
Electronics Manufacturing and Equipment	$2,501,822,021
Business Associations	$2,454,165,598
Oil & Gas	$2,317,233,106
Miscellaneous Manufacturing and Distributing	$1,878,785,962
Hospitals/ Nursing Homes	$1,794,639,211
Education	$1,772,523,038

Direct Lobbying focuses on influencing legislation through the communication with a legislator or government official. *Grass Roots Lobbying* focuses on influencing legislation through an attempt to affect the opinions of the public or any segment of the public.

NOTE: In 2010, the U.S. Supreme Court struck down two campaign finance provisions that limited independent political expenditures by corporations and other organizations and placed aggregate limits on individual donations. The Court found that the provisions infringe on the right of free speech and that the aggregate limits do not prevent a narrowly defined version of corruption.

Social Media Influence

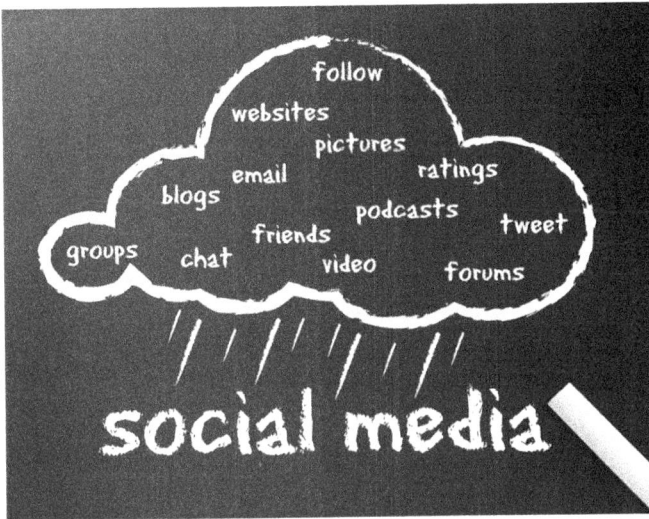

Compared with 2018, a larger share of social media users in the U.S. now say their views about an issue changed because of something they saw online

% of U.S. adult social media users who say they have changed their views about a political or social issue because of something they saw on social media in the past year

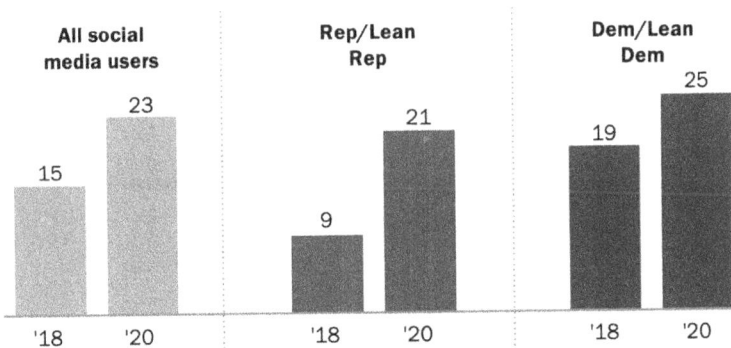

All social media users		Rep/Lean Rep		Dem/Lean Dem	
15	23	9	21	19	25
'18	'20	'18	'20	'18	'20

Note: Those who did not give an answer are not shown.
Source: Survey of U.S. adults conducted July 13-19, 2020.

PEW RESEARCH CENTER

Religious Influence

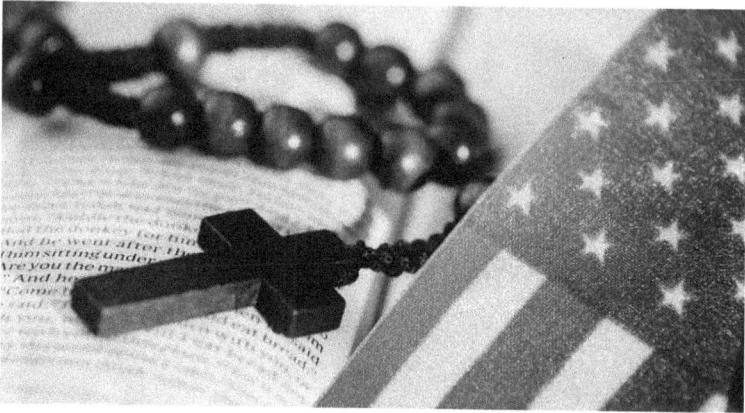

Half of Americans say Bible should influence U.S. laws; 28% favor it over the will of the people

Bible should have____ influence on U.S. laws

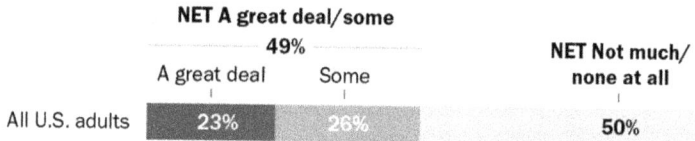

	NET A great deal/some 49%		NET Not much/none at all
	A great deal	Some	
All U.S. adults	23%	26%	50%

If Bible and will of people conflict, which should have more influence on U.S. laws?

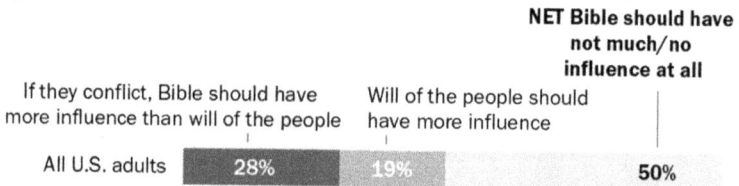

	If they conflict, Bible should have more influence than will of the people	Will of the people should have more influence	NET Bible should have not much/no influence at all
All U.S. adults	28%	19%	50%

Note: Figures may not add to subtotals indicated due to rounding. Those who did not answer are not shown.
Source: Survey conducted Feb. 4-15, 2020, among U.S. adults.
"White Evangelicals See Trump as Fighting for Their Beliefs, Though Many Have Mixed Feelings About His Personal Conduct"

PEW RESEARCH CENTER

Socio-political Influence

Dealing with COVID-19 outbreak among top policy priorities for both parties

% of U.S. adults who say ___ should be a top priority for the president and Congress to address this year

	Rep/ Lean Rep	Dem/ Lean Dem	Rep- Dem diff
Addressing issues around race	24 ●	● 72	**-48**
Dealing with global climate change	14 ●	● 59	**-45**
Dealing with coronavirus outbreak	60 ●	● 93	**-33**
Dealing with problems of poor people	35 ●	● 68	**-33**
Reducing health care costs	46 ●	● 67	**-21**
Addressing criminal justice system	35 ●	● 56	**-21**
Improving education	43 ●	● 61	**-18**
Improving transportation	27 ● ● 36		**-9**
Improving job situation	63 ● ● 71		**-8**
Dealing with drug addiction	24 ●● 30		-6
Improving political system	60 ●● 64		-4
Dealing with immigration	39 ●39		0
Securing Social Security	51 ●● 54		+3
Dealing with global trade	29 ●● 35		+6
Strengthening economy	75 ● ● 85		**+10**
Defending against terrorism	58 ● ● 68		**+10**
Reducing crime	39 ● ● 55		**+16**
Strengthening military	28 ● ● 51		**+23**
Reducing the budget deficit	29 ● ● 54		**+25**

Note: Significant differences in **bold**.
Source: Survey conducted Jan. 8-12, 2021.

PEW RESEARCH CENTER

Influence of Wealth and Income Inequality

"Over the past 40 or so years, the American economy has been funneling wealth and income, reverse Robin Hood-style, from the pockets of the bottom 99 percent to the coffers of the top 1 percent. The total transfer, to the richest from everyone else, amounts to 10 percent of national income and 15 percent of national wealth."

—Christopher Ingraham, Reporter, February 6, 2018, The Washington Post

Since 1981, the incomes of the top 5% of earners have increased faster than the incomes of other families

Average annual change in mean family income, by income quintile and for the top 5%

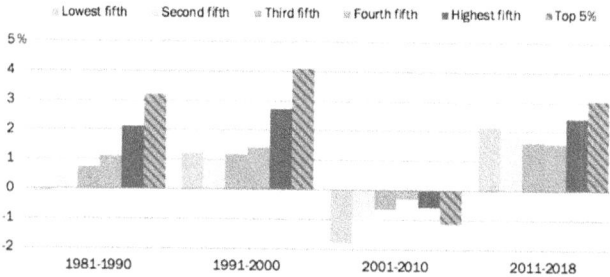

Note: Estimates of change from 2011-2018 are affected by revisions to the Current Population Survey in 2014. See Methodology for details.
Source: U.S. Census Bureau, Historical Income Tables, Table F-3.
"Most Americans Say There Is Too Much Economic Inequality in the U.S., but Fewer Than Half Call it a Top Priority"

PEW RESEARCH CENTER

The gaps in wealth between upper-income and middle- and lower-income families are rising, and the share held by middle-income families is falling

Median family wealth, in 2018 dollars, and share of U.S. aggregate family wealth, by income tier

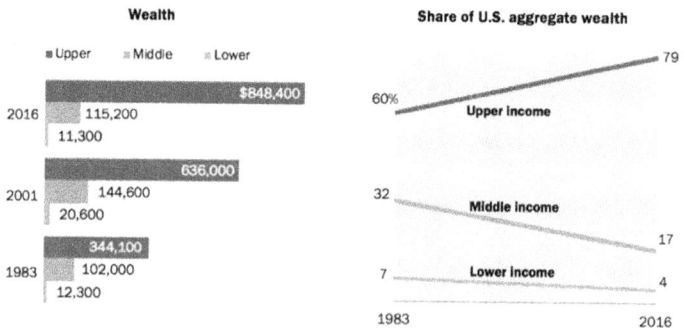

Note: Families are assigned to income tiers based on their size-adjusted income.
Source: Pew Research Center analysis of the Survey of Consumer Finances.
"Most Americans Say There Is Too Much Economic Inequality in the U.S., but Fewer Than Half Call it a Top Priority"

PEW RESEARCH CENTER

Influence of the Less Educated

"Education, not surprisingly, makes an important contribution to the acceptance of political compromise in the US. At a moment of great polarization in American politics, with bipartisanship hard to come by in policy making, political dialogue characterized more by outrage than civility, and politicians rewarded by voters more for "sticking to their guns" than for reaching consensus, we believe – and many educated people agree – that we could use more compromise and less intransigence."
—James M. Glaser, Jeffrey M. Berry and Deborah J. Schildkraut, Political Research Quarterly, August 16, 2019

Percent Who Prefer Compromise By Educational Attainment

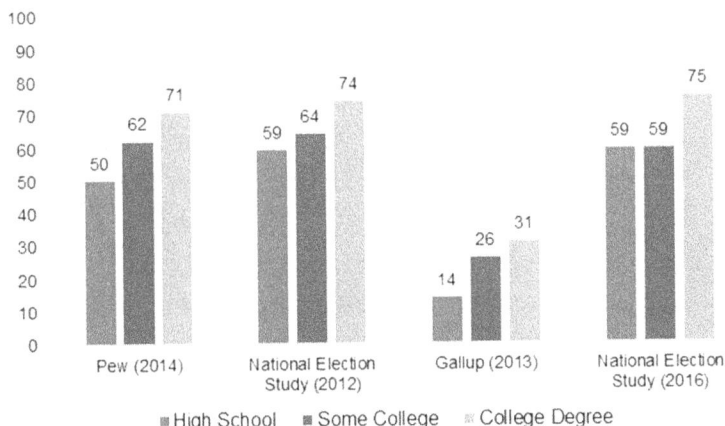

	High School	Some College	College Degree
Pew (2014)	50	62	71
National Election Study (2012)	59	64	74
Gallup (2013)	14	26	31
National Election Study (2016)	59	59	75

Research Quarterly

Less-educated Americans more inclined to see some truth in conspiracy theory that COVID-19 was planned

% of U.S. adults who think the theory that the coronavirus outbreak was intentionally planned by powerful people is ...

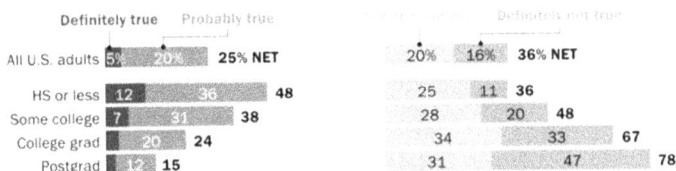

	Definitely true	Probably true	NET			Definitely not true
All U.S. adults	5%	20%	25% NET	20%	16%	36% NET
HS or less	12	36	48	25	11	36
Some college	7	31	38	28	20	48
College grad		20	24	34	33	67
Postgrad		12	15	31	47	78

Pew Research Center

We ardently believe that an impartial and honest review of just a portion of the sophisticated *ecosystem* of organized *societal influence* within America, like the review you have just performed, sufficiently makes the case for the *magnitude* and intensity of its *invasiveness*.

In the following nine chapters, we further substantiate the invasiveness and carefully examine the societal influences that have historically *factored* into and still play a significant role in the *framing*, *feeding* and *fertilizing* of the present-day social and political landscape in America.

Unquestionably, there are many factors, which can contribute to the spread of preferences, beliefs and desires in the tissues of American culture. However, our research led us to find nine factors that we believe are the most invasive in America today.

The nine *Primary Factors* are:

- The Influence of *The Human Mind*
- The Influence of *Selfishness*
- The Influence of *Apathy and Indifference*
- The Influence of *The Less Educated*
- The Influence of *Social Media and Mass Misinformation*
- The Influence of *Conspiracy Theories*
- The Influence of *Partisan Politics*
- The Influence of *Wealth and Power*
- The Influence of *Religious Hypocrisy*

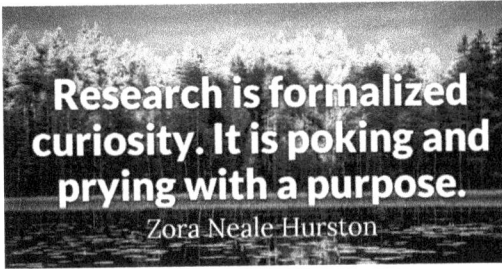

Research is formalized curiosity. It is poking and prying with a purpose.
Zora Neale Hurston

As our research progressed, we became convinced that a deeper examination of the *rationale* and *impacts* of each of these *Primary Factors* was necessary. It was our belief that a deeper examination of each factor would expose the degree of influence that each has on many aspects of America's social, economic and political constructs. We also believed that this type of constructive analysis could shed considerable light on the answer to the question — *Why is it so hard to become a people person in America?*

During the yearlong and sometimes *jaw-dropping* examination, we were somewhat surprised by the transparency and availability of the evidence verifying many of our assumptions. About halfway through the research period, we were reminded of a quote by the award-winning novelist, Margaret Atwood who once said, *"The best way of keeping a secret is to pretend there isn't one."* In the end, we both felt that we indeed had accomplished our mission and gained a greater appreciation of *why it is so hard to become a people person.*

We also gained some great insights into what we can do to embrace and contribute to America's humanity more deeply. We believe that a curious and thoughtful read of the remaining chapters will offer you the opportunity, to do likewise.

CHAPTER TWO

The Human Mind

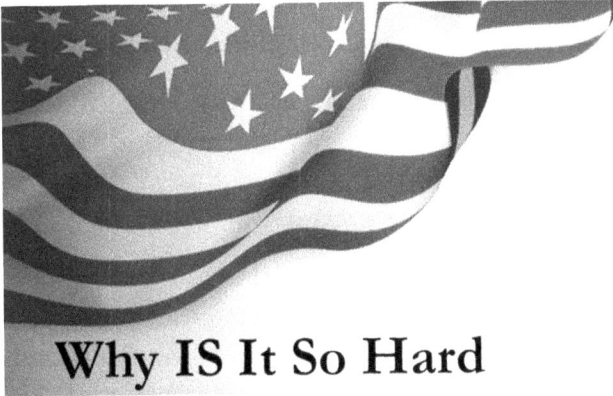

The Influence of The Human Mind

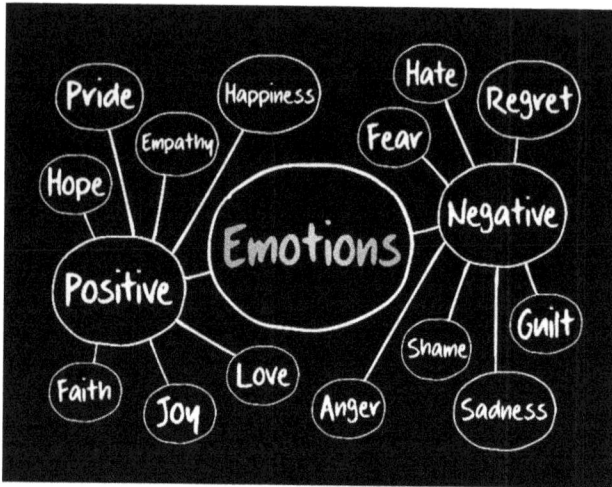

s Alia Crum, an assistant professor of psychology and director of the Stanford Mind and Body Laboratory said in a recent interview, *"Our minds aren't passive observers, simply perceiving reality as it is. Our minds actually change reality"*.

We have spent many years reading the books and studying the works of some of the world's most renowned psychologist. For those of you who have a similar interest in understanding how the human brain and mind works, what we are about to say will not be a surprise. As human beings, much of what we think and most of our thoughts, *"arise in our conscious experience without us knowing how it got there"*, and *"the mental work that produces impressions, intuitions, and many decisions goes on in silence in our mind"*.

Both insights into how the human mind functions are taken from the work of Daniel Kahneman, the Professor of Psychology and Public Affairs Emeritus at Princeton's Woodrow Wilson School of Public and International Affairs. His book titled, *Thinking Fast and Slow* is a New York Times bestseller, and according to William Easterly of the Financial Times is *"one of the greatest and most engaging collections of insights into the human mind I have read"*.

In line with Kahneman's work, the Distinguished University Professor of Philosophy at the University of Maryland, College Park, Peter Carruthers, who is an expert on the philosophy of the mind, empirical psychology and cognitive neuroscience, outlines many of his ideas on conscious thinking in his 2015 book titled, *The Centered Mind: What the Science of Working Memory Shows Us About the Nature of Human Thought*. In the book, Carruthers insists that *"conscious thought, judgment and volition are illusions*—[They] *arise from processes of which we are forever unaware"*.

Carruthers adds, *"In neurophilosophy, however, we refer to "thought" in a much more specific sense. In this view, thoughts include only nonsensory mental attitudes, such as judgments, decisions, intentions and goals. These are amodal, abstract events, meaning that they are not sensory experiences and are not tied to sensory experiences. Such thoughts never figure in working memory. They never become conscious. And we only ever know of them by interpreting what does become conscious, such as visual imagery and the words we hear ourselves say in our heads"*.

Our goal here is not, to attempt to present all the relevant aspects of neuroscience, or to expect you to become an expert in the study of the complexities of the human mind. The reality is that, as we worked on untangling the factors that we believe influences why it is so hard to become a *people person*, the *human mind,* and how it functions, stood out as one of the most significant factors.

We consider the insights discussed above to be remarkable. This is not only because these insights shed light on why, so many people seem to gravitate toward other people, *who think the way they do,* and *have the same beliefs.* But also, because the immense research into how the human mind works, strongly indicates that we do not know how we arrived at our preferences, prejudices, opinions, fears and intuitive beliefs.

In his book, Kahneman also indicates that, *"As we navigate our lives, we normally allow ourselves to be guided by impressions and feeling, and the confidence we have in intuitive beliefs and preferences is usually justified.*

But not always. We are often confident even when we are wrong, and an objective observer is more likely to detect our errors than we are".

EXERCISE. Here is an exercise that may give you a better sense of just how difficult it can be at times for us to detect our own *errors*. Below is a sample list of news stories that could be easily found on any media platforms in 2020 and 2021. Take a few minutes to read each of them carefully. You may recall seeing some of these news stories during the period they were published. The question is: *How many of them do you believe to be true versus misinformation or fake news?* They all seem to be what you might expect to hear and read within America's culture today.

A Sample of News Headlines Influencing the American People's Mindset

- June 10, 2021 - *A bipartisan group of senators released a report on the security and intelligence failures related to the Jan. 6 attack on the U.S. Capitol "singles out" former President Trump for inciting…the riots.*

- April 23, 2021 - *An alternate juror in the trial of Derek Chauvin said she initially had "mixed feelings" about jury duty, because of concerns about "disappointing" either side and the possibility of "rioting". She said she "would have said guilty".*

- April 1, 2021 - *The shooter accused of killing 10 people in Boulder, Colorado, came to the U.S. "illegally from Mexico and purchased the firearm from a guy that sells stolen guns".*

- March 10, 2021 - *The attack on the U.S. Capitol on Jan. 6 was not an "armed" insurrection. FBI testifies that no guns were seized from suspects that day.*

- November 20, 2020 - *Philadelphia mob boss Joseph "Skinny Joey" Merlino stuffed ballot boxes for Joe Biden and the Democrats — and would testify about the scheme in exchange for a presidential pardon.*

When you read Chapter Six, *The Influence of Social Media and Mass Misinformation,* you will find the answers. You may be surprised by some of the answers to this question unless you have already performed some fact-checking on these news stories and messages.

As Kahneman's research indicates, it is not easy for us to detect the errors in our own thoughts and intuitive beliefs.

However, as we will discuss in the following Chapters, there are many *objective observers* within our society today, who can detect the errors in our thoughts and intuitive beliefs, and not all the *observers* have our best interest in mind. In fact, most of them feed on our *inability* to evaluate and understand the source of thoughts and beliefs to further their own personal, professional and economic interest.

The Impact of the Influence of *The Human Mind*

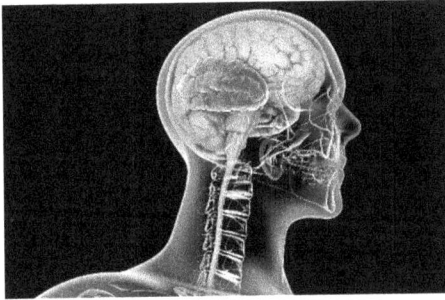

We all should take the time to understand how our mind really works and how the *influence of the human mind* unknowingly *frames how we think*. Unless we do so, our capability to identify the natural errors in judgement and choice, in others and in ourselves will persist. We will also continue to be vulnerable, and this deceptive influence will continue to impact our ability to become *people persons*.

An Approach to Counter the Impact

First, take the time to sit down and make a list of all your strongest thoughts, and beliefs.

Remember, beliefs are a slippery concept, and some of your beliefs maybe cultural values that are learned and shared across groups. Mistaken or speculative beliefs are sometimes difficult to distinguish and can sometimes be so hard to change.

Be honest. If you have the slightest inclination that you may have a certain thought or belief --- put it on your list. For example, you may think that you are not prejudice in some manner but can honestly say that you do *feel different* when you are in a specific environment and around particular people.

Then, consciously make the effort to seek intervention. The intervention may require multiple discussions with an objective third party. It should NOT be a spouse, friend or family member. It may require the help of a psychiatrist. The goal is to identify distorted beliefs, understand how they formed, and learn to be more skeptical of your own thoughts and beliefs.

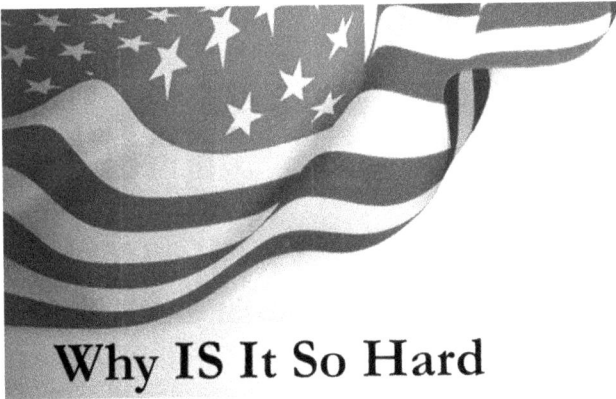

CHAPTER THREE
The Influence of Selfishness

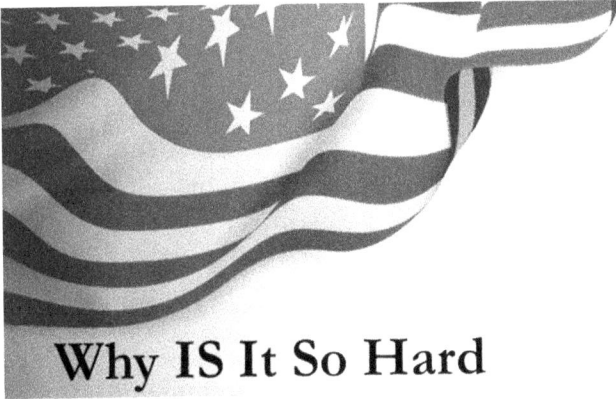

The Influence of Selfishness

MASKS REQUIRED

THANK YOU FOR YOUR COOPERATION

"Self·ish | \ 'sel-fish- concerned excessively or exclusively with oneself : seeking or concentrating on one's own advantage, pleasure, or well-being without regard for others." — **Merriam-Webster's Unabridged Dictionary**

In an article titled, *"Selfishness Is Learned"*, written in June 2016 in the Culture/Psychology section of the Nautilus Magazine, Matthew Hutson discussed the work performed by the great Enlightenment philosopher Jean-Jacques Rousseau and Thomas Hobbes, a 17th-century English philosopher, which included ten experiments to help determine the "default mode" of most people: *selfishness* or *selflessness?*

Rousseau and Thomas documented their breakthrough in their 17th-century experimentation as follows:

"When your default is to betray, the benefits of deliberating — seeing a chance to cooperate — are uncertain, depending on what your partner does. With each partner questioning the other, and each partner factoring in the partner's questioning of oneself, the suspicion compounds until there's zero perceived benefit to deliberating. If your default is to cooperate, however, the benefits of deliberating — occasionally acting selfishly — accrue no matter what your partner does, and therefore deliberation makes more sense.

So, it seems there is a firm evolutionary logic to the human instinct to cooperate but adjust if necessary—to trust but verify. We ordinarily cooperate with other people, because cooperation brings us benefits, and our rational minds let us decipher when we might occasionally gain by acting selfishly instead...We tend to be cooperative — unless we think too much... Most of us are genuinely good. And if we're not, we can be encouraged to be. The math is there."

While reviewing this work, we found the research and the evidence discovered to be quite comforting. The fact that there is a *"firm evolutionary logic to the human instinct to cooperate"* is fundamental to our ability, as humans, to become *people persons*.

Then, as we dug a little deeper, we thought that we should examine some more contemporary research to determine if the discovery by the 17th-century work of Rousseau and Thomas has been corroborated and re-enforced in recent studies.

During our examination, we discovered an extensive and widely respected study released in January 2017. It was published in the *Annual Review of Psychology* and titled, *Social Motivation: Costs and Benefits of Selfishness and Otherishness*. The study was undertaken by Jennifer Crocker, Amy Canevello, and Ashley A. Brown — Professors within the Department of Psychology at The Ohio State University. In their study they examined recent evidence regarding the consequences of *selfishness* and what they called *"otherishness"* for psychological well-being, physical health, and relationships. In the research they focused on several intrapsychic mechanisms such, as positive and negative affect, self-esteem and self-efficacy, a sense of meaning and purpose in life, and a sense of connectedness to or isolation from others.

What we found most interesting and aligned with our research regarding the role that the influence of *selfishness* plays in erecting barriers to the average American becoming a *people person*, is in their conclusion. They summarized the conclusion of their study as follows:

"Are people basically selfish? People give and take in social relationships; they have the capacity to be both selfish and otherish. Indeed, people are hardwired for both self-interest and other-interest; in

the face of threats to existence, the survival of the individual sometimes depends on the human capacity for self-interest.

A fight-or-flight motivational system that promotes looking out for oneself can save lives in some circumstances. Yet, the survival of the species depends on the evolved human capacity to care for others.

Humans have evolved to live cooperatively in social groups in which people take care of each other. Accordingly, it makes sense that people are psychologically constructed in such a way that giving to others can be rewarding despite its obvious material costs, and selfishness can be costly despite its immediate material benefits."

Most of us would agree that during the arrival of the coronavirus pandemic in the United States in 2020, *we the people* revealed both *genuine goodness* and *human capacity to care for others.* However, we also revealed an increased level of *selfishness* associated with America's culturally diverse and polarized society — a society struggling with 21st-century social, environmental and political change. As we mentioned in the Introduction:

"After a few months of watching the news stories, we could not dismiss and had to seriously question the undeniable display of selfishness, hatred, political polarization and healthcare disparities within American society — even during a national crisis."

As we began to correlate our research into the role that the influence of *selfishness* plays in erecting barriers to becoming a *people person*, we were drawn to an insightful realization.

That is, the realization that with most of us being *genuinely good* people, there must be something within our nation's social institutions that *discourages* versus *encourages* the level of social cooperation required to maintain a more civil, cooperative and humanitarian society. As a humanitarian society, Americans would tend to sacrifice for a *common good*, when it's most needed — like during a ravishing coronavirus pandemic, which has thus far taken the lives of over four million people globally with over 600,000 of those being the lives of Americans.

We also discovered an interesting argument on how some of America's social institutions may *encourage* a degree of selfishness. This argument was set forth in a series of articles published in *Psychology Today* by Thomas Henricks, Ph.D., Professor of Sociology Emeritus at Elon University. In the articles, Dr. Henricks suggests that America's key social institutions may *encourage* a private and even selfish vision of life, which make it more difficult for Americans to place a higher value on *societal* and *public good*. We have summarized his thoughts in the table below.

Does American Society Encourage Selfishness?
Our Social Institutions Support a Preoccupation With Self

Institution	Encourages Individualism
Family Life	The quest for independence and individualism dominates the typical American family structure and relationship. From the selection of a spouse and child rearing, to moving to where the jobs are, and the search for individual quality of life experiences, it's all about *"me"* and *what I want* and *what I can do.*
Education	Schools teach habits of industriousness, self-discipline and individuality. As an *individual*, I should do my own work honestly and receive judgment solely for what I do.
Healthcare	There are societies that consider healthcare a universal right that government policies must support. The American society is not one of those. *"I am expected to fend for myself."* However, "better" jobs provide better healthcare for families, while tens of millions have no coverage.
Legal Justice	Although there are certain exceptions for crimes committed by dependent children, for the most part, *individuals* bear responsibility for their own acts in courts of law. Sounds reasonable, especially in an individualistic society — *but the ability to acquire the best lawyer "individualizes" justice.*
Religion	Faith communities, which hold their members to common standards and emphasize serious moral purposes, are at one level a great bulwark *against the selfish spirit.* However, it is notable that most of these churches stress the importance of *individual morality*, as opposed to *the obligations of groups or even of society itself.*

Thomas Henricks, Ph.D., Professor of Sociology Emeritus at Elon University, June 2021

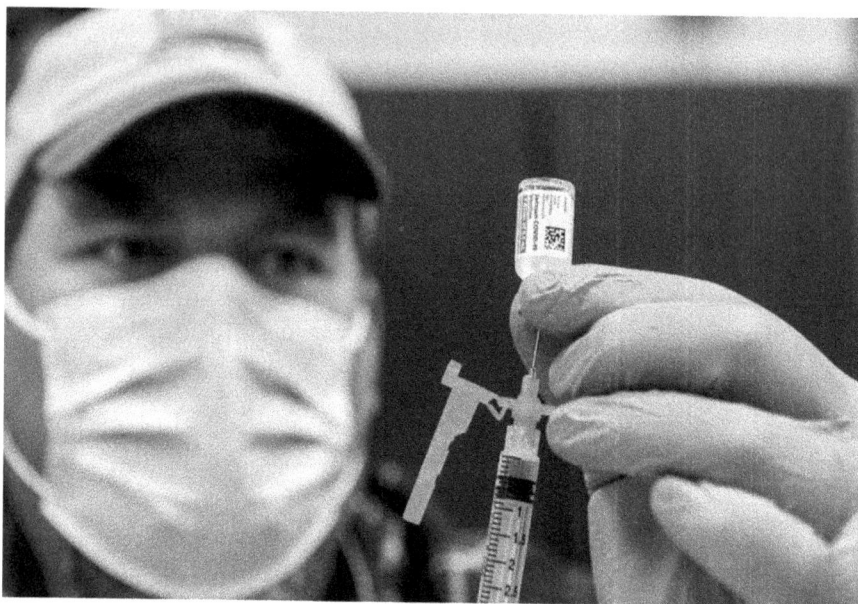

Photo by Joseph Prezioso/AFP via Getty Images/TNS

- **COVID-19 Vaccine Hesitancy: Understandable and Irrational**
  — Marie McCullough, The Philadelphia Inquirer, April 27, 2021

- **GOP Governor Says It's Time To Blame The Unvaccinated For Pandemic Surge**
  — Ed Mazza, Overnight Editor, HuffPost, July 23, 2021

- **How Society Got Broken: The Age of Selfishness and Narcissism**
  — Nnaemeka Ugochukwu, Eco Warrior Princess, July 23, 2019

Without any doubt, *seeking or concentrating on one's own advantage, pleasure, or well-being without regard for others*, has been the focus of many studies and much research across the globe for centuries. When viewed from the prospective of its role in a modern society, there is also little doubt that very few economic and social problems can be addressed without a broad level of public cooperation, compromise and a sense of humanity.

The media headlines sighted above indicates that within the American society today, even during a pandemic that has claimed twice the number of American lives lost in World War II, a hugely unexpected number of Americans are reluctant to unselfishly do what is needed for the *common good*. One of the headlines also suggests that the level of selfishness today, has reached the point where it deserves the label, *The Age of Selfishness and Narcissism*.

For the sake of all Americans and humanity in general, we certainly hope that the humanitarian actions of the majority of Americans are far from what is needed to claim such a label. Mainly because of what we mentioned in our discussion in Chapter One: *Humanity, and a humanitarian culture have transformative forces which can lay the foundation for, resolving issues within societies that selfishness, celebrity, wealth, politics, threats, coercion, regulations, laws, punishment or physical destruction have failed to do, since human existence.*

The Impact of the Influence of *Selfishness*

Commenting on the many economic and social problems that American society now confronts, *Newsweek* columnist Robert J. Samuelson recently wrote: *"We face a choice between a society where people accept modest sacrifices for a common good or a more contentious society where groups selfishly protect their own benefits."*

In our research, we noted that for decades in America, appeals to the *common good* have surfaced in discussions of a company's social responsibilities, climate change, the lack of investment in education and solutions to problems of crime and poverty. It appears that a governing majority of Americans claim that the country's most fundamental social problems grow out of a lack of commitment to the *common good*, coupled with an equally widespread pursuit of individual interests. Yet, *we the people*, continue to elect candidates who obviously have chosen to become and sustain careers as partisan politicians.

Yes. We agree that moving the nation toward more *selflessness* and collectively responding to pressing societal problems and issues is a formidable challenge.

However, as individuals, we believe that seriously understanding the significant impact that the *influence of selfishness* has on *preventing unity, maintaining a more contentious society,* and *framing how we think,* is a great place to start.

An Approach to Counter the Impact

One of the best approaches we all can take to move toward being less selfish is to develop a higher level of empathy or *putting ourselves in someone else's shoes.* Obviously, you will not be able to actually walk in someone else's shoes. However, you can make the effort to consciously think about the other people around you and consider how they might be impacted before you take an action. The more you practice empathy and consider what other people are going through, the sooner you will be able to contribute to the *common good* of an American society, we all must live in.

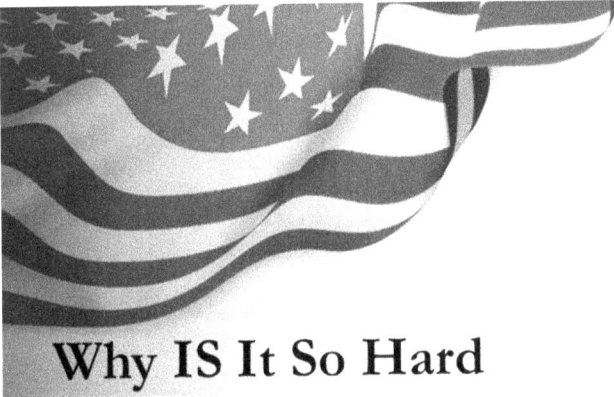

Why **IS** It So Hard

CHAPTER FOUR

The Influence of Apathy and Indifference

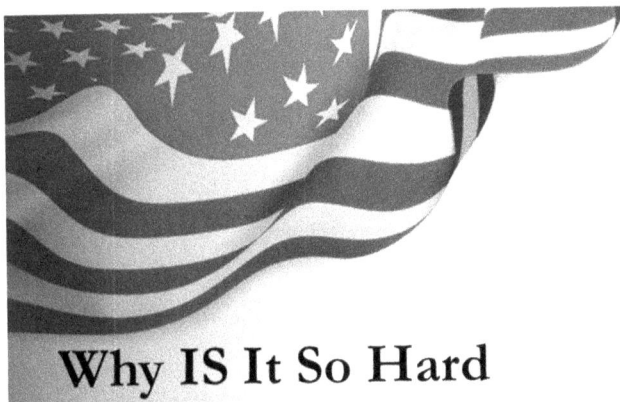

Why **IS** It So Hard

The Influence of Apathy and Indifference

"**Apathy** *is the absence or suppression of passion, emotion, or excitement. When adding the social aspect to this, it creates a negative connotation. Not only is one absent of their own life's situations, they care even less about the situations of others — even if they can do something about it. Social apathy is a desensitization of humane involvement where society is concerned.*"

"**Indifference** *is the human condition of not caring about or being interested in something or someone.*"

As we mentioned in the Introduction, we began this journey after reflecting upon the automobile incident back in April 2020, and being reminded of Jim, the *people person*, whose single action made us feel a real sense of *community* during crisis.

With the backdrop of our characterization of a *people person* as "*an individual …striving to bring out the best in oneself, as a human being and respecting the uniqueness and the humanity of others*", we continued our journey by focusing on the challenges presented by *social apathy* and the apparent *indifference* of many Americans toward the need to participate in civic activities, to ensure that we have the *public governance* needed, to produce the *results* that meet our country's economic needs, as well as the humanitarian needs of the American society.

During our efforts to untangle the primary causes of why many individuals chose not to sufficiently participate in civic activities vital to keeping check on our democracy, and sustaining social unity, we found a puzzling combination of possibilities.

However, we observed that national news reports on the reasons why many continue to express a hesitancy to take the life-saving vaccines to help eradicate the COVID-19 pandemic, provides some interesting insights into the cause of some of the *social apathy* and *indifference*. Here are some representative headlines.

GOP governor's vaccination tour reveals depths of distrust
By Andrew Demillo, AP News, July 17, 2021

"Woods, 67, introduced himself … as "anti-vax" and said that he thinks there are too many questions about the effects of the vaccine and that he doesn't believe the information from the federal government about them is reliable."

Poll Reveals Who's Most Vaccine-Hesitant in America and Why
By Cara Murez, HealthDay Reporter, April 29, 2021

"Vaccine hesitancy is emerging as a key barrier to ending the COVID-19 pandemic. Our study [limited to working-age adults] indicates that messaging about COVID-19 vaccine safety and addressing trust are paramount", said lead author Wendy King, associate professor of epidemiology in the University of Pittsburgh Graduate School of Public Health.

Exploring Barriers to COVID-19 Vaccination and Reasons for Vaccine Hesitancy
By Daniel Richardson, HERO Registry, July 1, 2021

"There are many reasons people list for not getting the COVID-19 vaccination. Several reasons include:

- *Fears about the vaccines' safety and how quickly they were developed.*
- *Belief that the vaccines could give you COVID-19 or make you sick.*
- *Belief that COVID-19 would not cause serious illness.*
- *Personal right to opt out.*
- *General opposition to vaccines."*

Why Some People Don't Want a Covid-19 Vaccine
By David Robson, BBC, July 22, 2021

"Social media is rife with posts disparaging the vaccine hesitancy – but these reactions to a complex and nuanced issue are doing more harm than good."

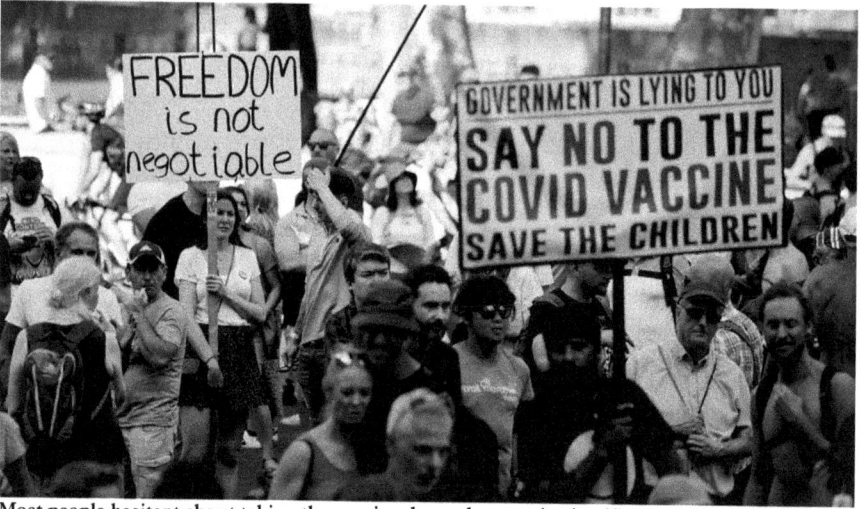

Most people hesitant about taking the vaccine do not have anti-scientific views like the small minority of anti-vaccine protesters (Credit: Tolga Akmen/AFP/Getty Images)

It appears that at the heart of much of the vaccine hesitancy, and maybe much of the *social apathy* and *indifference* in America, is the *lack of trust* — in American governmental institutions and in each other as *we the people*.

In a March 2021 report by the Deloitte Global, the authors shared the following, regarding what they called *a crisis of trust*:

"In the United States, trust in the federal government was at only 20% in August 2020—a slight increase from 2019 (17%), but still near historic lows. This is not a recent phenomenon — public trust in the US federal government has been declining for decades."

"A majority of citizens also say they are dissatisfied with how the federal government has handled the pandemic. Even trust in state and local governments, which have traditionally enjoyed a higher level of public trust, significantly declined during the pandemic. A recent Deloitte survey of 4,000 Americans found that citizens' perception of their trust in the US federal government was the lowest in comparison with state and local government and other commercial entities."

As we began to conclude our research into the *social apathy* and the apparent *indifference* of so many Americans, and its impact on discouraging societal unity and respecting the humanity of others, the reality surrounding COVID-19 vaccine hesitancy, and other supporting research, led us to suspect *deficiencies* within three vital *threads* of America's *Social Fabric*, as the probable root cause. The three threads are:

- An erosion of *Social Capital*.
- The lack of sufficient *Social Cohesion; and*
- The lack of a consensus on the *Social Pillars* or *essential support structures* required in a thriving 21st century America.

The following is a brief and insightful discussion of each of these *fundamental threads*. We believe a thoughtful review of their purpose, and the critical role they collectively play in a democratic, civil and humanitarian society will shed some light on how, shortfalls, can lead to *social apathy* and *indifference*.

The first two excerpts regarding *social capital* and *social cohesion* are from a presentation published recently by Investopedia.

Social Capital

"Social capital allows a group of people to work together effectively to achieve a common purpose or goal. It allows a society or organization, such as a corporation or a nonprofit, to function together as a whole through trust and shared identity, norms, values, and mutual relationships."

- Social capital refers to the internal social and cultural coherence of society. It has been described as a lubricant that facilitates getting things done and allows people to work together, and to access benefits from social relationships.

- Our society, economy, institutions, and political system could not exist without social capital. Social capital refers to the internal social and cultural coherence of society. As such, social capital has been described as a glue.

- For individuals, social capital is important because it is an important source of power and influence that helps people to *get by* and *get ahead*. The adage: *"it's not just what you know, but who you know"*, relates to the powerful effects and importance of social capital.

- For groups and organizations, social capital is vital to their efficiency and even existence. Social capital enables people to work together and facilitates cooperation and innovation.

- Any organization that doesn't consider the importance of social capital is missing an opportunity for improvement, and risking inefficiencies and peril.

Social Cohesion

- For society, social capital is also important as it allows societal institutions to exist, and it maintains the coherence of society.

  "Social cohesion refers to the extent of connectedness and solidarity among groups in society."

- Social cohesion is a social process, which aims to consolidate plurality of citizenship, by reducing inequality, socioeconomic disparities and fractures in the society.

Social Pillars

By *Social Pillars*, we are referring to the essential *social structures* required, to support a democratic society, whose *rules of interactions*, uphold humane social conditions. We discussed the importance of a society's *rules of interactions* in Chapter One.

Our research in this area discovered a well-respected and widely discussed depiction of such a structure within an essay written by Robert P. George and Herbert W. Vaughan, Senior Fellow of the Witherspoon Institute. The essay is titled, *"The Five Pillars of a Decent and Dynamic Society"*. It was originally published in the book titled, *The Thriving Society: On The Social Conditions of Human Flourishing.*

We have summarized an overview of the *five pillars* from the essay below.

The Five Pillars of a Decent and Dynamic Society

Pillars	Overview
Respect for the Human Person	*"To be just, a society must be built upon the recognition that all human beings have dignity simply because they have rational faculties that allow them to know, love, reason, communicate, and flourish as community members."*
Sexuality and Family	*"The institution of the family is built upon the comprehensive sexual union of man and woman. No other institution can top the family's ability to transmit what is pivotal — character formation, values, virtues, and enduring love — to each new generation."*
Politics and Law	*"As we learn from Aristotle, man is the political animal because he is the rational animal — the speaking animal who gives and receives reasons for his actions. This makes engagement in politics natural for humankind."*
Education and Culture	*"Schools and universities transmit the knowledge, wisdom, and values of their society, thus acting as bearers of tradition. No society can maintain its coherence or existence without a place for tradition in education."*
Business and Economics	*"Business and economics are built upon concern for the common good and the ways in which the economic order contributes to — or detracts from — human flourishing."*

From *The Thriving Society: On The Social Conditions of Human Flourishing*
The Witherspoon Institute, 1st edition January 1, 2015

"Well, Doctor, what have we got—a Republic or a Monarchy?"

"A Republic, if you can keep it."

"Mrs. Powel of Philadelphia reportedly asked the above question to Benjamin Franklin, who had taken part in the secret deliberations of the Constitutional Convention of 1787. His response underscores the responsibility that citizens have in maintaining this experiment known as The United States of America, the success of which rests upon civic engagement."

Benjamin Franklin

The Impact of the Influence of
Apathy and Indifference

As we mentioned earlier, our characterization of being a *people person* embodies an *approach* to living *one's life*. Our research clearly has shown that the role of civic engagement and participation within a democratic republic is critical in determining *one's quality of life*.

While concluding our research of the rationale and impacts that the influence of *apathy* and i*ndifference* play in erecting barriers to becoming a *people person*, we identified what we believe to be a *common factor*, which causes many Americans to become disengaged from two of the most important virtues of human life — *kindness* and the seeking of *humanity*.

Our research identifies this *common factor* as the inability of many Americans, to *care*. A *caring society*, as we conceive it, is one in which *care* penetrates all major social institutions.

Since *caring* is the freely given commitment from the heart of one to another, the *lack of humanitarian perspective* within the vital threads of the American *Social Fabric*, we just discussed — namely, *Social Capital, Social Cohesion* and *Social Pillars* — can propagate *social apathy* and *indifference* throughout our country's diverse and geographically dispersed communities.

An Approach to Counter the Impact

Most scholars think that one of the most effective approaches to countering the impact of *apathy* and *indifference* is for all Americans to make a personal commitment to become engaged in civic activity within their local community. Consistent with the African proverb, *"It takes a village to raise a child"*, American history has shown that the best way to maintain a safe, healthy, and civil republic is for local communities of people, to become socially involved, and to interact positively with each other. During our research, we discovered a sound and straight forth approach for improving civic engagement, as set forth in a book by Thomas Ehrlich, titled, *Civil Responsibility and Higher Education.* In his work, Ehrlich lists the following as *actions* that can be taken, and *values* that should be embraced, to become effectively engaged in helping to create the public governance required for a more *humane* and *caring* society.

Actions

- ✓ *Political participation through voting, voter registration, or being an election judge.*
- ✓ *Educating Americans on government and history.*
- ✓ *Volunteering in organizations that build community well-being.*
- ✓ *Advocating for legislation and models.*
- ✓ *Representing fellow citizens by appointment or election.*

Values

- ✓ *Trusting and respecting how a community wants to take action for itself.*
- ✓ *Creating agency and power in people, particularly those most affected by an issue.*
- ✓ *Nurturing or fostering healthier, stronger, happier places to live.*
- ✓ *Engaging community members in a process that affects them and their communities.*
- ✓ *Promoting transparency and participation.*

CHAPTER FIVE

The Influence of
The Undereducated

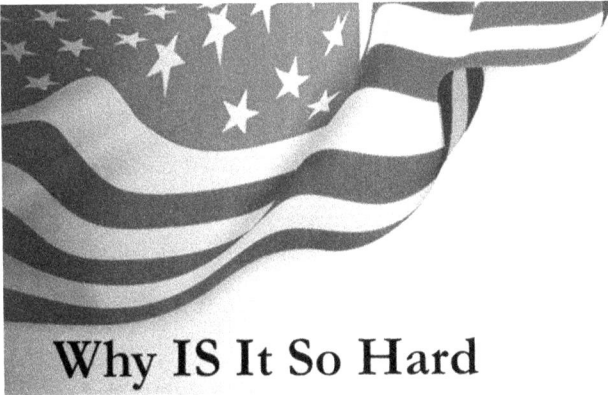

Why IS It So Hard

The Influence of The Less Educated

"In the year of Trump and Brexit, education has become the greatest divide of all – splitting voters into two increasingly hostile camps. But don't assume this is simply a clash between the ignorant and the enlightened. On 23 February, [Former President] Donald Trump stood before a rally of cheering supporters to celebrate a thumping victory in the Nevada Republican caucus – his third consecutive win, in defiance of the naysayers who had predicted that his bubble was about to burst."

"If you listen to the pundits, we weren't expected to win too much – and now we're winning, winning, winning the country," he bragged. "We won with young. We won with old. We won with highly educated. We won with poorly educated. I love the poorly educated."

— **From an article titled, "How the Education Gap is Tearing Politics Apart" by David Runciman, October 16, 2016**

A s we mentioned in the Introduction, our mission is to discuss, examine and attempt to untangle many of the issues and other *societal matters* that we believe have and continue to contribute to the growing challenge of becoming a *people person* in America. When the *Influence of the Less Educated*, initially appeared on our list of possible *Framing Factors* or *influences*, which creates barriers to becoming a *people person*, it was not clear as to how one portion of the American population *being less educated than* another, could create such barriers.

However, as we dug deeper beneath the surface, we found a growing number of public incidents, recent surveys and somewhat surprising, yet very transparent references, such as the comments above taken from the article, *How the Education Gap is Tearing [American] Politics Apart*, by David Runciman. Former President Trump's bragging comments, illuminate the reality, that it is not *the less educated*, but those who use the *lack of public knowledge* and *factual*

103

awareness of certain groups of citizens, to their own personal, and political advantage to create, disunity, within the American society.

In the following sections we will briefly discuss how education is often used to shape *social identity* and *frame* our understanding of ourselves and our relationships with others — both of which has an impact on efforts to *strive to bring out the best in oneself, as a human being and respecting the uniqueness and the humanity of others.*

Education and a Democratic Society

"Education is one of the most important predictors – usually, in fact, the most important predictor – of many forms of social participation – from voting, to associational membership, to chairing a local committee to hosting a dinner party or to giving blood. The same basic pattern applies to both men and women and to all races and generations. Education, in short, is an extremely powerful predictor of civic engagement."

— **David Edward Campbell, Department of Political Science, University of Notre Dame, Symposium on Social Outcomes of Learning, March 24, 2006**

Most Americans would agree that education is important in the functioning, of a successful democratic society. As Franklin D. Roosevelt once said, *"Democracy cannot succeed unless those who express their choice are prepared to choose wisely. The real safeguard of democracy, therefore, is education."*

Our research indicates that from our nation's founding, it has been the belief that, *we the people,* need to be educated to maintain a thriving Republic. A knowledgeable, informed and involved people affects society in many important ways. To think that *education* can become a fundamental divide in our democracy, with the *educated on one side* and the *less educated on another*, may be alarming to some. However, we found that on many fronts, that there is a growing partisan divide in the view of the value, of higher education.

A 2012 survey by the Pew Research Center indicates that only half of American adults think colleges and universities are having a positive effect on the way things are going in the country these days. About four-in-ten (38%) say they are having a negative impact – up from 26% in 2012.

The Highly Educated

We believe that to most Americans, being *highly educated*, means *having extensive information or understanding of the world and possessing more formal education, as associated with college and university degrees.*

According to the Pew Research Center, *highly educated adults* – particularly those who have attended graduate school – are far more likely than those with less education, to take predominantly *liberal positions* across a range of political values. They also indicate that these differences have increased over the past two decades.

Adults with postgraduate experience most likely to have consistently liberal political values

% with political values that are...

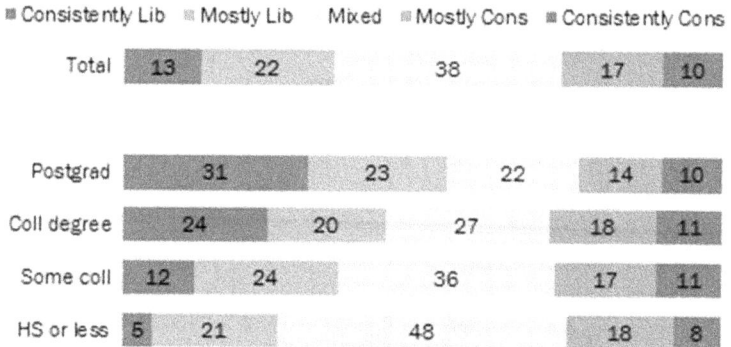

■ Consistently Lib   ■ Mostly Lib   Mixed   ■ Mostly Cons   ■ Consistently Cons

	Consistently Lib	Mostly Lib	Mixed	Mostly Cons	Consistently Cons
Total	13	22	38	17	10
Postgrad	31	23	22	14	10
Coll degree	24	20	27	18	11
Some coll	12	24	36	17	11
HS or less	5	21	48	18	8

Source: Survey conducted Aug. 27-Oct. 4, 2015 (N=6,004). Ideological consistency based on a scale of 10 political values questions.

PEW RESEARCH CENTER

It is generally believed that most Americans who lean liberal, support social programs, labor unions, consumer protection, workplace safety regulation, equal opportunity, disability rights, racial equality, regulations against environmental pollution, and criminal justice reform.

The Less Educated

We also believe that to most Americans, being *less or poorly educated* means *having less formal education, possibly without a high school education, and possessing a lesser understanding of the world as compared to the average knowledge of others.*

In recent surveys by the Pew Research Center, *"The majority of adults who do not have a college degree (72% of the public in 2015), far fewer express liberal opinions. About a third of those who have some college experience but do not have a bachelor's degree (36%) have consistently liberal or mostly liberal political values, as do just 26% of those with no more than a high school education. Roughly a quarter in each of these groups (28% of those with some college experience, 26% of those with no more than a high school education) have consistently conservative or mostly conservative values."*

It is also generally believed that most conservatives, support free-market capitalism, restrictions on immigration, increased military, lower taxes, spending, gun rights, restrictions on abortion, deregulation, and restrictions on labor unions.

According to a survey of U.S. adults, conducted during the peak of the COVID-19 pandemic June 4-10, 2020, by the Pew Research Center, *less educated* Americans were more inclined to be *rigidly partisan,* and see some truth in conspiracy theories, such as the one which surfaced indicating that COVID-19 was planned.

Less-educated Americans more inclined to see some truth in conspiracy theory that COVID-19 was planned

% of U.S. adults who think the theory that the coronavirus outbreak was intentionally planned by powerful people is ...

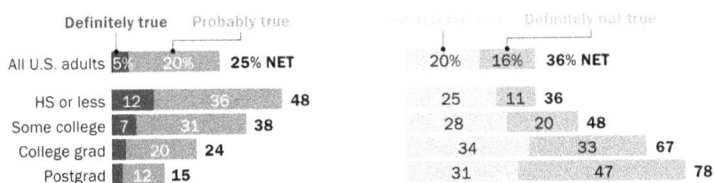

	Definitely true	Probably true	NET			Definitely not true	NET
All U.S. adults	5%	20%	25% NET	20%	16%	36% NET	
HS or less	12	36	48	25	11	36	
Some college	7	31	38	28	20	48	
College grad		20	24	34	33	67	
Postgrad	12	15		31	47	78	

Does not show respondents who declined to answer the question or who said they were not sure whether the theory is true.
Source: Survey of U.S. adults conducted June 4-10, 2020.

Pew Research Center

The Impact of the Influence of *the Less Educated*

Question #1 : Do you ever wonder why, so many working-class and mostly *less educated* Americans voted for Donald J. Trump in 2016 and continue to approve of him even after the "Big Lie" *[that Trump won the 2020 election]*, the brazen and violent January 6, 2021 insurrection on the U.S. Capital led by Trump supporters, and after the fact that, as President he supported a health care bill that would disproportionately hurt them?

Question #2 : Do you ever wonder why, so many *highly educated* professionals who tend to lean Democratic, routinely support Democratic presidential campaigns, even though Republican tax policies would probably leave more money in their pockets?

Most experts believe the answer to both questions, is *partisanship.* Our research indicates that *Party affiliation* has become an all-encompassing identity that outweighs the details of specific policies. In their 2020 book titled, *"The Limits of Party: Congress and Lawmaking in a Polarized Era"*, James M. Curry and Frances E. Lee write: *"Partisan identification is bigger than anything the party does."*

"Partisan alignment and the resulting antipathy are deeper and more extensive – than at any point in the last two decades. These trends manifest themselves in myriad ways, in politics and in everyday life. And a new survey of 10,000 adults nationwide finds that these divisions are greatest among those who are the most engaged and active in the political process."

Source: 2014 Political Polarization in the American Public, The PEW Research Center

Research also indicates that the higher levels of *partisanship* within the American society today, stems from something much more fundamental. It stems from *certain people's* idea of who they *are.* We found that even though this partisanship is pervasive through the American society, as noted in recent Pew Center Surveys, a large and growing number of the *less educated* population within our society are becoming *more partisan* and even *more rigid* in their positions. Thus, their *influence* on erecting barriers to a more *unified* and *humanitarian* society is significant and growing.

An Approach to Counter the Impact

Our research discovered several efforts of Social Psychologists to address conflict among groups in America and develop solutions that can help these groups come together.

One approach that we believe has significant merit is one that was set forth in a July 2, 2019, article titled, *What Are the Solutions to Political Polarization?* by Lee De-Wit, Sander Van Der Linden and Cameron Brick published in the Great Good Magazine.

They introduce their approach with the following:

"While there might be various political seeds that have helped drive the recent spike in polarization, it has gotten to a point where polarization is being exacerbated by some of the psychological processes that shape how we interpret identity and groups. This is a significant point to understand because it highlights that if we are to address polarization, we need to think not just about political solutions, but also solutions that are grounded in our understanding of social psychology."

Here is an overview of the Five Point Approach they have set forth to tackle the issue of political polarization. We believe this type of approach, could possibly help counter, the growing impact of the *Influence of the Less Educated,* caused by the group's *rigid partisanship* and *opposition to compromise* for the nation's greater good.

1. **Intergroup Contact.**

   The "contact hypothesis" suggests that getting to know each other can reduce prejudice between groups. One promising civic model for enabling more meaningful contact between groups in conflict involves, "Citizens Assemblies," where representative citizens are brought together to deliberate over, challenging social, or political issues.

2. Perspective Taking.

Perhaps one of the most important aspects of contact is that it might enable one to see things from another's perspective.

3. Superordinate Goals.**

One of the best solutions from the psychological literature is that identity-based conflicts require common goals or a "superordinate" sense of identity to bring people back together.

4. Proportional Voting.

While searching for psychological solutions to polarization, it's important not to ignore the context in which political decisions are made, and to think about the way in which different political systems will engage with, and exacerbate, aspects of our psychology. The U.S. is one of the few countries to be dominated by just two political parties. This fact is almost certainly a reflection of a, "winner take all", voting system. Many countries employ a proportional (or mixed) system, which means that if a party gets 5 percent of the popular vote, they will receive 5 percent of the seats in a given representative body.

5. Voting for Policies, Not for Parties.

Another potential solution to identity-based policy preferences is to hold direct referendums on specific issues. Among large territories, California and Switzerland both regularly use referendums to address complex policy topics.

Of course, **superordinate goals also come with a potential risk. Whenever we form an in-group, we also create out-groups. As Richard Dawkins once tweeted:

"National pride has evil consequences. Prefer pride in humanity. German pride gave us Hitler, American pride gave us Trump, British pride gave us Brexit. If you must have pride, be proud that Homo sapiens could produce a Darwin, Shakespeare, Mandela, Einstein, or Beethoven."

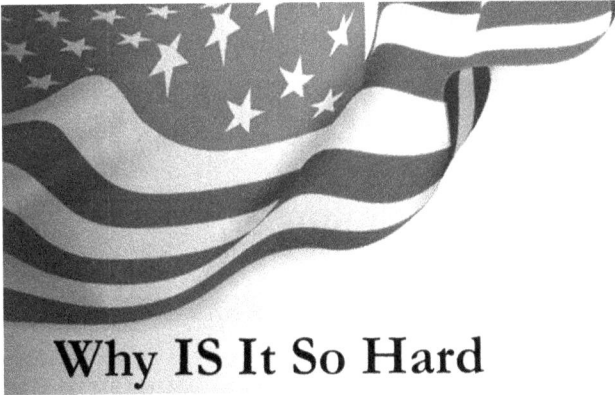

CHAPTER SIX

The Influence of
Mass Misinformation

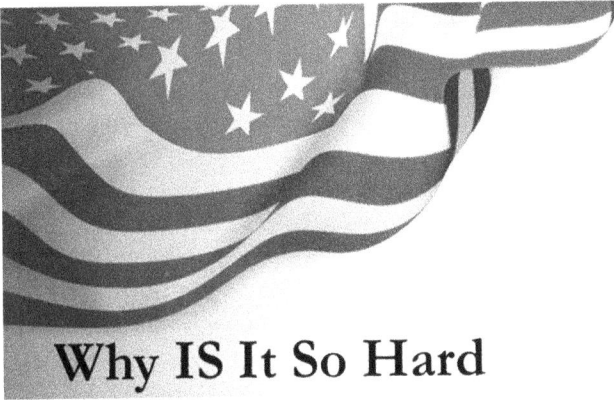

Why IS It So Hard

The Influence of Social Media and Mass Misinformation

"FactCheck.org is one of several organizations that works to debunk misinformation shared on the social media networks. They provide a guide on how to flag suspicious stories on Facebook and a list of websites that have carried false or satirical articles, as well as a video and story on how to spot false stories."

Here are five of the many fake news stories that FactCheck.org has debunked and reported on in 2020 and 2021.

Facebook Post Misleads on Bipartisan Capitol Attack Report and Interview

June 10, 2021

On June 8, a bipartisan group of senators released a report on the security and intelligence failures related to the Jan. 6 attack on the U.S. Capitol. The report did not "single out" former President Donald Trump "for inciting ... the riots," as a Facebook post from the advocacy group Occupy Democrats could lead social media users to believe.

Posts Mislead on Words of Alternate Juror in Chauvin Trial

April 23, 2021

An alternate juror in the trial of Derek Chauvin said she initially had "mixed feelings" about jury duty, because of concerns about "disappointing" either side and the possibility of "rioting." She said she "would have said guilty," but as an alternate did not participate in the verdict. Social media posts now use her words to erroneously imply that a juror admitted outside pressure was a factor in the verdict.

Unfounded Claims About Colorado Gunman

April 1, 2021

A social media post is spreading baseless claims that the shooter accused of killing 10 people in Boulder, Colorado, came to the U.S. "Illegally from [M]exico and purchased the firearm from a guy that sells stolen guns." Law enforcement officials say the suspect came to the U.S. from Syria as a child, and the gun used was legally purchased.

Capitol Protesters Were Armed With Variety of Weapons

March 10, 2021

Conservative social media posts misleadingly claim the attack on the U.S. Capitol on Jan. 6 was not an "armed" insurrection, citing FBI testimony that no guns were seized from suspects that day. But 23 people have been charged with having deadly or dangerous weapons during the assault — including a loaded handgun found on a man arrested on Capitol grounds.

Bogus Report Claims Philly Mob Boss Stuffed Ballot Boxes

November 20, 2020

A dubious website claims without evidence that Philadelphia mob boss Joseph "Skinny Joey" Merlino stuffed ballot boxes for Joe Biden and the Democrats — and would testify about the scheme in exchange for a presidential pardon. Merlino's attorney denies the claim, which originated on a website operated by a self-described "pro-Trump" political consultant.

As just mentioned, the news stories and messages listed in the prior pages and in the exercise introduced in Chapter Two, were all *debunked* by FactCheck.org and found to be misinformation or fake news. We are sure that most of you are not surprised.

According to Emily Thorson, a political scientist at Syracuse University and co-author of the book, *Misinformation and Mass Audiences*:

"Misinformation is false information that's out there in the world — anything from rumors to deliberate propaganda to unintentional errors. Disinformation, as we see it, is about the intention of the distributor. While misinformation may not be intended to deceive, disinformation is distributed intentionally and often strategically."

Mass misinformation is one of the biggest problems facing America today and plays an important role in influencing what we think, as well as how we relate to each other as a people. Social networking was once considered as a new and most efficient method to connect *people* to *people*. Then, what seems like overnight, social networking transformed into social media.

What is the difference you ask? You are not alone. Most people don't know the difference between social networking, and social media.

Social Media connects *people* to *people* and *people* to *content*. This transition over that last decade was the key to the sales strategy of products like Facebook, Twitter, and YouTube. It is also the main reason these platforms are dominating global markets in mass communication.

Outside of connecting *people* to *people* and *people* to *content*, products like Facebook, YouTube and Twitter depend on other organizations, companies and individuals to deliver additional data to their platforms. Thus, increasing the scale in their enormous data infrastructure across their global networks, and the internet. These companies became viable businesses, and influencers by using mapping, aggregating, and tracking tools which allow them to sell data obtained from interactions of social networks, or to monetize those relationships as advertising, targeted posts, and promoted messages.

The bottom line for the companies is profits and huge asset valuations. In accordance with recently distributed data from *Statista* , a German company specializing in market and consumer data, in 2020, Facebook and YouTube had over two billion active users and Google dominated the market financially with over $180 billion in annual revenue.

The Impact of the Influence of
Social Media and Mass Misinformation

As result, without us being consciously aware, the influence of strategically disseminated misinformation and disinformation has a significant impact on many aspects of our lives, and our ability to move toward a more humanitarian society.

When we constantly hear, read and share, in our daily lives, misinformation or disinformation, it has a way of becoming *reality* in our minds. It also creates the prospect for us to *narrow* our focus on the actual social, and economic issues affecting us as a nation and *widens* our propensity to demonize, resent, and even hate others in our society who we believe are the cause of our hardship.

Unknowingly, and sometimes maliciously, social media, and mass misinformation drives misguided inhumane thoughts, group think, unfounded beliefs, partisanship, conspiracy theories, discrimination, the exploitation and exacerbation of divisions in society, as well as the erosion of long-standing institutional doctrine. All of which play major roles in inhibiting our ability to become *people persons*.

An Approach to Counter the Impact

It is difficult for us as individuals to do much to stop the dissemination of misinformation, and fake news.

However, we can do some important things that are in our control to minimize the impact it has on our lives and our humanity. We can avoid being a *super spreader*, by fact checking what we hear and what we read. Also, before we share something on Twitter or Facebook, we should assess the origin, credibility and authority of the source of that news or information.

Just as important, we should work on increasing our overall mindfulness and remembering that *we as individuals are responsible for our actions toward others*. This reality is a critical starting point for moving toward becoming a *people person*.

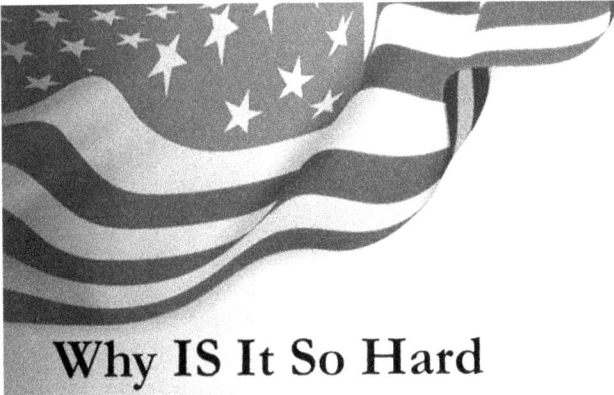

Why IS It So Hard

CHAPTER SEVEN

The Influence of
Conspiracy Theories

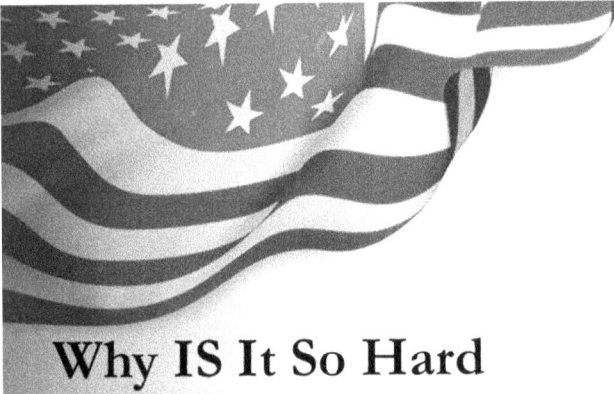

Why **IS** It So Hard

The Influence of Conspiracy Theories

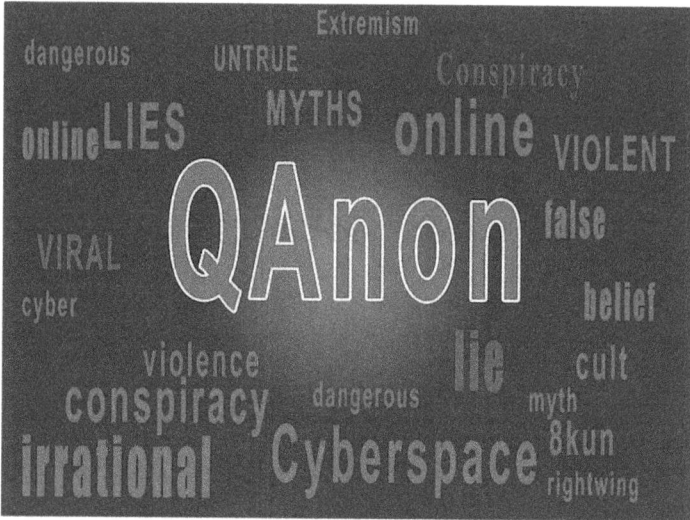

"In a culture fueled by burnout, a culture that has run itself down, our national resilience becomes compromised. And when our collective immune system is weakened, we become more susceptible to viruses that are part of every culture because they're part of human nature - fearmongering, scapegoating, conspiracy theories, and demagoguery."

— **Arianna Huffington, American Journalist**

In Chapter one, we introduced the work of Daniel Kahneman, the Professor of Psychology and Public Affairs Emeritus at Princeton's Woodrow Wilson School of Public and Int'l Affairs at Princeton, and his book titled, *Thinking, Fast and Slow.*

Kahneman is recognized as one of the world's experts on how the human brain and mind works. In all of our research for this book, we found his comments, on how the mind works, to be the most profound. We believe that just to know that most of our thoughts, *"arise in our conscious experience without us knowing how it got there"* and *"the mental work that produces impressions, intuitions, and many decisions goes on in silence in our mind,"* should give all of us reason to always *"think harder and deeper"* about societal events, that seem *unbelievable* to most Americans, yet *totally believable* and even rational, by an outspoken, and publicly influential minority segment of the U.S. population.

According to Katherine Schaeffer, a research analyst at Pew Research Center and a June 2020 Pew Research Center survey, *"Most Americans (71%) have heard of a conspiracy theory circulating widely online that alleges that powerful people intentionally planned the coronavirus outbreak. And a quarter of U.S. adults see at least some truth in it – including 5% who say it is definitely true, and 20% who say it is probably true. The share of Americans who see at least some truth to the theory differs by demographics and partisanship."*

Less-educated Americans more inclined to see some truth in conspiracy theory that COVID-19 was planned

% of U.S. adults who think the theory that the coronavirus outbreak was intentionally planned by powerful people is ...

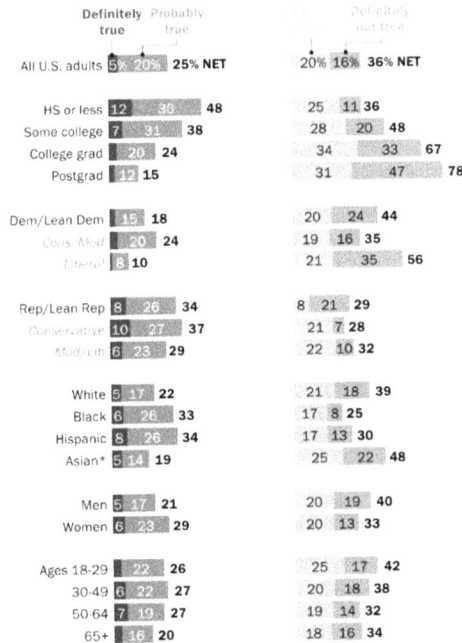

	Definitely true / Probably true		Definitely not true	
All U.S. adults	5% 20%	25% NET	20% 16%	36% NET
HS or less	12 36	48	25 11	36
Some college	7 31	38	28 20	48
College grad	20	24	34 33	67
Postgrad	12	15	31 47	78
Dem/Lean Dem	15	18	20 24	44
Cons. Mod	20	24	19 16	35
Liberal	8	10	21 35	56
Rep/Lean Rep	8 26	34	8 21	29
Conservative	10 27	37	21 7	28
Mod/Lib	6 23	29	22 10	32
White	5 17	22	21 18	39
Black	6 26	33	17 8	25
Hispanic	8 26	34	17 13	30
Asian*	5 14	19	25 22	48
Men	5 17	21	20 19	40
Women	6 23	29	20 13	33
Ages 18-29	22	26	25 17	42
30-49	6 22	27	20 18	38
50-64	7 19	27	19 14	32
65+	16	20	18 16	34

*Asian adults were interviewed in English only.
Note: Does not show respondents who declined to answer the question or who said they were not sure whether the theory is true. White, Black and Asian Americans include those who report being only one race and are not Hispanic. Hispanics are of any race.
Source: Survey of U.S. adults conducted June 4-10, 2020.

PEW RESEARCH CENTER

Jacob Chansley, a.k.a. the QAnon Shaman, speaks on January 06, 2021, in Washington
— Getty Images

On May 27, 2021, Chuck Todd, Mark Murray and Carrie Dann provided the following briefing, from "Meet the Press" and the NBC Political Unit:

"Washington, we have a problem — politically, informationally and societally, when 15 percent of Americans agree with the QAnon statement that the U.S. government, media and financial worlds, are controlled by a group of Satan-worshipping pedophiles who run a global child sex trafficking operation."

— or, when 20 percent agree with this statement: *"There is a storm coming soon that will sweep away the elites in power and restore the rightful leaders."*

— or, when another 15 percent agree that *"Because things have gotten so far off track, true American patriots may have to resort to violence in order to save our country."*

The reporting is based on the results of a study by the *Public Religion Research Institute (PRRI)*, which was conducted online March 8-30, 2021. The study also indicates that *"Republicans, those who trust far-right news outlets like OANN and Newsmax, and white evangelicals, and Hispanic Protestants, are all more likely to believe these statements than other Americans."*

With twenty percent of all Americans believing in the *QAnon* and the *coronavirus outbreak* conspiracy theories, we, and most likely many other Americans, feel that it is very difficult to just call *this part* of our culture, *fringe*.

As we moved further into our research on the role that the *Influence of Conspiracy Theories* may play in framing the perspective of those Americans, we began to give more thought to Arianna Huffington's insightful comment, that we shared at the beginning of this Chapter, and her belief that, *conspiracy theories*, are a part of human nature.

In a June 29, 2017, Research Article titled, *Conspiracy Theories as Part of History: The Role of Societal Crisis Situations*, the authors, Jan-Willem van Prooijen, and Karen M Douglas shared the following:

"Contrary to common assumptions, belief in conspiracy theories has been prevalent throughout human history. Historical incidents suggest that societal crisis situations — defined as impactful and rapid societal change that calls established power structures, norms of conduct, or even the existence of specific people or groups into question — have stimulated belief in conspiracy theories. Evidence suggests that the aversive feelings that people experience when in crisis — fear, uncertainty, and the feeling of being out of control — stimulate a motivation to make sense of the situation, increasing the likelihood of perceiving conspiracies in social situations. After being formed, conspiracy theories can become historical narratives that may spread through cultural transmission."

After months of insightful research on the *Influence of Conspiracy Theories,* we arrived at an overall conclusion, which agrees with the premise of the van Prooijen and Douglas publication, and Arianna Huffington's belief — *conspiracy theories*, are a part of human nature.

At this point, we began to ponder two questions.

First, what are the *societal crisis situations* that history will record for the conspiracy theories thriving within the American society today?

Secondly, what tangible impact does the *presence* and *societal distractions* of the most politically inspired conspiracy theories have on those Americans who desire to become *people persons*.

Our research led us to believe that the three primary *societal crisis situations,* that might contribute to most of the conspiracy theories thriving within the American society today, are as follows.

I.   The growing intellectual and wealth divide in our country today.

With the growing intellectual and wealth divide in the United States today, a higher percentage of Americans now depend too heavily upon their *intuition* to guide their beliefs, thoughts and partisan preferences.

A surprising insight, that our research uncovered in this regard, is the fact that most Americans in this category are not aware of the extent of this growing divide in our country. In a March 31, 2015, Scientific American article titled, *Economic Inequality: It's Far Worse Than You Think: The great divide between our beliefs, our ideals, and reality,* Nicholas Fitz wrote:

"The average American believes that the richest fifth own 59% of the wealth, and that the bottom 40% own 9%. The reality is strikingly different. The top 20% of U.S. households own more than 84% of the wealth, and the bottom 40% combine for a paltry 0.3%. The Walton family, for example, has more wealth than 42% of American families combined."

Relying mostly on one's *intuition* is the less stressful way for most Americans to cope with major, and complex issues, like *global warming, systemic racism* and *immigration.* Stress is decreased when one does not have to *think deeply* or use their *"system 2 thinking",* the most analytical part of the brain, as described by Daniel Kahneman, in his book, *Thinking, Fast and Slow.*

Because *believing* is an *instinct,* intuition is how many Americans control and manage stress. This is particularly important in times of uncertainty. According to Eric Oliver, Professor of Political Science at the University of Chicago, *"They [intuitionist] go with their gut. They're attracted to symbols and metaphors. They orient their understanding of the world based on what they're feeling, over scientific beliefs."*

II. The changes in America's workforce, social behaviors, environment and political polarization.

These changes have produced opportunities for more societal, and governmental *suspicion,* by an increasing number of Americans, due to four conditions, we believe may be viewed, as part of a *societal crisis.*

- The changing makeup of America's diverse workforce and America's inability, to execute a plan, to make the shifts needed to replace good jobs, for middle America, displaced by the 21st century economy.

- Recognizable climate change, resulting in the increase of forest fires, summer temperatures and hurricane damage.

- The uncontrollable rise in healthcare cost and the burden on a larger number of middle-income Americans; and

- The extreme polarization within the U.S. Government caused by growing, and relentless partisanship. The mostly, politically driven divide, that has created a political ecosystem, incapable of compromise, and the ability to address complex national issues such as, *national healthcare, immigration, social security, social justice reform, fair elections and increasing income inequities.*

The result is an increasing number of Americans feeling as if they have *no control* of their environment or their future.

According to Rob Brotherton, author of *Suspicious Minds: Why We Believe Conspiracy Theories:*

"There are studies of people being deprived of control...and under those circumstances people engage more with superstitious kind of views. Not only that, but people are more likely to endorse conspiracy theories. These are all manifestations of our desire to understand our environment and feel like we can exert some control over it."

In our research, we learned that *most people just happen to be measurably more intuitive than others, meaning that they are also more prone to magical thinking and conspiracy thought. Scientists proved this connection by comparing one's level of apprehensive behaviors, like checking the locks on their doors frequently, with how much their emotions influenced decision-making, by asking whether a subject would rather do, something symbolically bad, or tangibly bad. People who avoid something that feels wrong but do not have a tangible negative consequence, are much more intuitive.*

III.   Social Media's significant role in the consumption and distribution of conspiracy theories.

The rise of social media has allowed for easier dissemination of conspiracy theories, according to a February 2021 report by the Global Network on Extremism and Technology. GNET is the academic research arm of the Global Internet Forum to Counter Terrorism.

With the pervasiveness and omnipresence of social media, it is now easier than ever to rapidly consume and distribute conspiracy theories. The ability of conspiracy theory *creators* and *sustainers* within today's more global, and sometimes, malicious landscape, is increasing and being rewarded with substantial profits and political advantage.

Even though our research did not find any reference describing *conspiracy theory's* relationship to *Social Media,* as a *societal crisis,* many believe that *QAnon* believers were involved in the shocking January 6, 2021, insurrection at the United States capital, where the 117th Congress was meeting to count the results of the Electoral College vote and certify the winner of the 2020 presidential election.

Darch Gregorian, Yahoo News, June 15, 2021

The Impact of the Influence of *Conspiracy Theories*

Our research did find that the *presence* and *societal distractions* of the *Conspiracy Theories*, do have tangible impacts on those Americans who desire to become *people persons*.

We believe that the findings of recent FBI report, Douglas and Uscinski Study 2019, *Culture Wars in America*, presents a set of challenges that can present true barriers to America becoming a more humanitarian society.

Here is a summary of the report's findings:

These [conspiracy] theories can have dangerous real-world ramifications:

- *Mass manipulation of public opinion.*
- *Increase in radicalized and extremist or violent behavior.*
- *Encourage targeting of specific people, places and organizations.*
- *Mainstreaming of fringe and debunked ideas and "junk science."*
- *Contribute to polarization of society.*
- *Undermine confidence in public leaders and institutions.*

An Approach to Counter the Impact

Conspiracy theories are captivating because they provide explanations for confusing, emotional and ambiguous events, when official answers, and explanations seem inadequate. Here is some insight which may help you *better understand* and *counter* your involvement in conspiracy theories. It is taken from an article in The American Psychiatric Association's publication, *Psychiatric Services*, titled, *Why Humans Are Vulnerable to Conspiracy Theories*. The article was written by Richard A. Friedman, M.D. and published in July 2020.

"Of course, not everyone is as vulnerable to conspiratorial thinking. Research shows that higher levels of education are inversely correlated with belief in conspiracies, presumably because education fosters critical thinking and skepticism, which makes it easier to suppress one's often misleading intuition."

CHAPTER EIGHT

The Influence of
Social Media

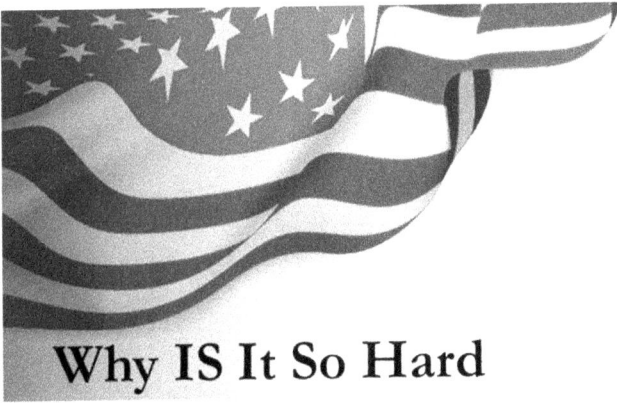

Why IS It So Hard

The Influence of Partisan Politics

**Most states send senators of the same party
to Congress**

Senate delegation by state, February 2021

■ Unified Democratic ■ Unified Republican ▨ Split

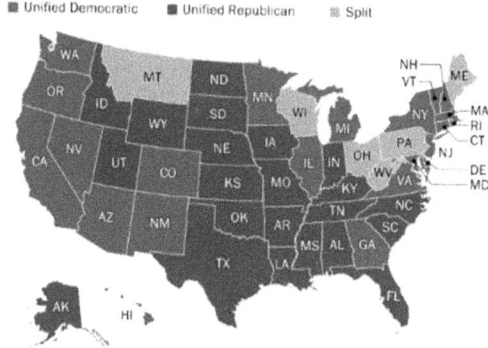

The Pew Research Center

A ccording to a recent Pew Research Center analysis, only six states now have U.S. senators of different parties – the smallest number of split delegations since Americans started directly electing their senators more than a century ago.

This was an interesting discovery that we found during our research into the *Influence of Partisan Politics,* as one of the primary factors, involved in framing American thought today. This finding left us wondering — *What does this tell us about where we are in 2021 compared to 1921, as a people, and as a society?*

It didn't take us long to begin to believe that *partisanship* or *a bias for one party or another,* might indeed psychologically impact an individual's *capacity for sympathy,* and the *ability to participate in the feelings, beliefs, and emotions* of other people. Why you ask?

First, let's examine two of the most important findings, namely, the fact that, *Partisanship Predates the U.S. Constitution,* and the reasons why, *American Politics and Political Polarization is Personal.*

Then, we will share our enlightened views on the impact that *Partisan Politics* has on an individual's efforts to become a *people person.*

Partisanship Predates The U.S. Constitution

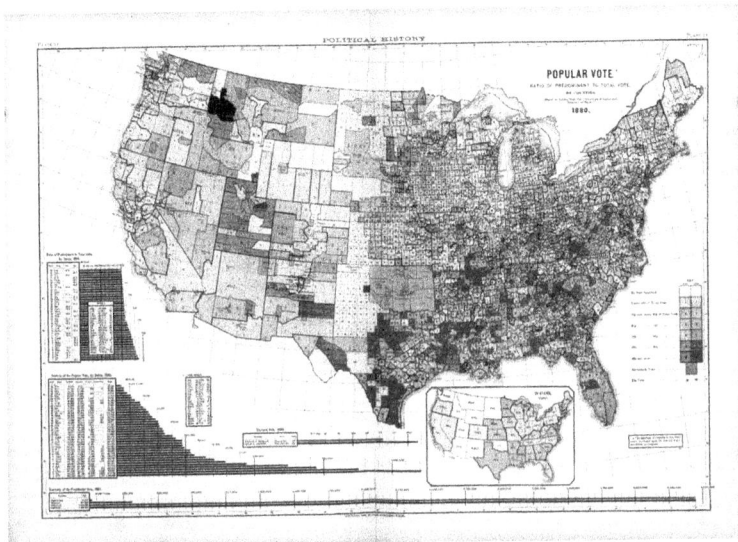

This 1880 presidential election map is the first to depict county-level results, revealing the depths of partisan division in the closest popular vote election in U.S. history. — Scribner's Sons, 1883. Geography and Map Division, Library of Congress, Washington, D.C.

As you may recall from your social studies classes in high school, the power of the *U.S. Federal Government* is held by, *we the people*. As Americans, we give power to the leaders we elect to represent us and serve our interests. The representatives are responsible for serving the interest of *all the people* in the country, and not just a few people. Also, as you are aware, it is the *U.S. Constitution,* which establishes our federal democratic republic form of government. It is called the *"supreme law of the land"* because no law may be passed that contradicts its principles, and no person or state government is exempt from following it.

Of course, as time goes on, it becomes more difficult to preserve such a governing structure while maintaining a federal government capable of responding to a changing world, full of unforeseen, domestic and global challenges. One source of the difficulty is working with our "fixed in stone" foundation, which is, of course, the U.S. Constitution.

This foundational document was written 240 years ago, when it was impossible to envision the matters facing today's America. To help with managing such difficulty, our country's founders established a process by which, the Constitution may be amended, and since its ratification, it has been amended 27 times.

However, as we have experienced over the past few decades, an even more perplexing difficulty to America's ability to address unforeseen, domestic and global challenges — such as, *national healthcare, immigration, global warming, social security, social justice reform, and increasing income inequalities* — has been the struggle associated with alleviating the mostly negative and paralyzing outcomes of *political partisanship.*

As we all know, political factions or parties were formed during the struggle over ratification of the U.S. Constitution in 1787. The friction between the parties increased, as the attention shifted, from the creation of a new *federal government* to the question of, the powers and the role, of U.S. Government.

The solution evolved into the reliance upon *we the people* to maintain *political parties,* and the *politics* required to debate, and resolve all conflicts regarding the sharing of control and power. It was envisioned that the *politics,* or activities between individuals and groups, would take the form of elected representatives working within the construct of constitutionally established *branches of the federal government* to arrive at the best compromised positions, to serve the interest of all the people, and ensure the survival of the Republic, while maintaining national unity.

We can only take comfort in knowing, that *political partisanship* has been an irritant for America's Republic since it was founded — as we partake, and for most of us, suffer through, the ultra-polarized partisanship of today. During a February 2016 National History Center briefing to the U.S. Congress, Donald Ritchie, historian emeritus of the Senate reminded the attendees that, *"George Washington had warned against political parties and partisanship in his farewell address."*

Unlike the process established in 1787, to amend and modernize the U.S. Constitution to address a changing world, positive changes in the outcomes of *political partisanship* in America, and *better* ways to address conflict in the role, and power of the federal government, must come from an America, with increasing numbers of, *better* people.

American Politics and Political Polarization is Personal

Liberals Want Walkable Communities, Conservatives Prefer More Room

Would you prefer to live in a community where ...

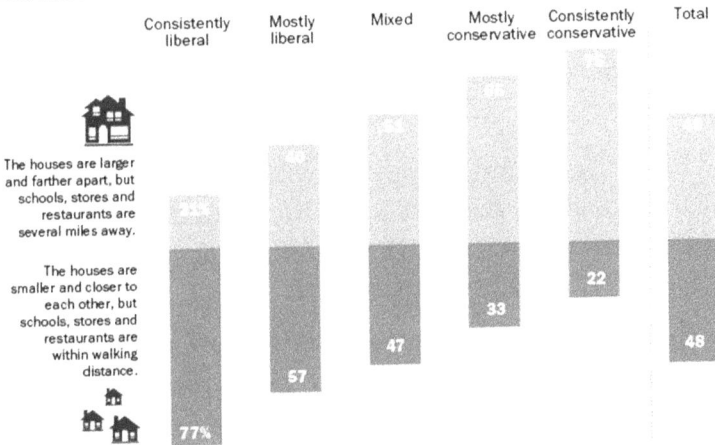

| | Consistently liberal | Mostly liberal | Mixed | Mostly conservative | Consistently conservative | Total |

The houses are larger and farther apart, but schools, stores and restaurants are several miles away.

The houses are smaller and closer to each other, but schools, stores and restaurants are within walking distance.

Consistently liberal: 77%
Mostly liberal: 57
Mixed: 47
Mostly conservative: 33
Consistently conservative: 22
Total: 48

Source: 2014 Political Polarization in the American Public
Notes: Ideological consistency based on a scale of 10 political values questions (see Appendix A). "Don't know" responses not shown.

PEW RESEARCH CENTER

In an insightful, New York Times opinion column, Thomas B. Edsall, Professor of political journalism, at Columbia University, shared the following:

"Political hostility in the United States is more, and more becoming personal hostility. New findings suggest that the sources of dispute, in contemporary life, go far beyond ideological differences, or mere polarization. They have become elemental, almost tribal, tapping into in-group loyalty and out-group enmity."

Our research on this topic, overwhelmingly supports that, in America today, *sources of dispute, in contemporary life, go far beyond ideological differences, or mere polarization.* As the 2014 study results reflected in the chart by Pew Research Center on the previous page confirms, *American politics and political polarization is indeed personal.*

If you have a tenancy to lean Liberal in your thinking, you most likely desire houses that are smaller, and located closer to each other, as well as prefer schools, stores, and restaurants that are within walking distance. If you are leaning Conservative, you most likely desire larger houses, that are located further apart, as well as prefer schools, stores, and restaurants that are miles away.

Of all our research into the personalization of politics, there were two findings that are both confirming, and concerning, regarding how political polarization, is a serious threat to America's humanity.

The first is found in a paper written in July 2014 by Shanto Iyengar, a political scientist at Stanford, and Sean Westwood, a post-doctoral researcher at Princeton. In the paper titled, *Fear and Loathing Across Party Lines,* they write:

"Hostile feelings for the opposing party are ingrained or automatic in voters' minds. Partisans now discriminate against their adversaries to a degree that exceeds discrimination based on race. We find that this discrimination pervades decision making of all kinds, from hiring to marriage choices."

Secondly, is a finding supported by a 2014 Pew Research Center study, which revealed that *"the level of antipathy that members of each party feel toward the opposing party has surged over the past two decades. Fully 36 percent of Republicans and 27 percent of Democrats believe the opposition party's policies, are so misguided that they threaten, the nation's well-being".*

We are reminded of an address given by Abraham Lincoln, later President of the United States, on June 16, 1858, at what was then the Illinois State Capitol in Springfield, where he said, *"A house divided against itself, cannot stand".*

The Impact of the Influence of *Partisan Politics*

As we said earlier, it didn't take us long to begin to believe that *partisanship* and *political polarization* might psychologically impact an individual's *capacity for sympathy*, and the *ability to participate in the feelings, beliefs, and emotions* of other people.

However, there *are* some benefits to *individuals* and *society* from *political polarization* and conflict, between opposing viewpoints, and there are many Americans who are benefiting.

They include these three groups:

- Individuals, organizations, and companies in the position to take advantage of, gain favor, or make money from, the behaviors of emotionally driven partisans who are seeking reinforcement for their views.

- Politicians who gain support, and maximize turnout when their constituents can be emotionally activated based on perceived threats, and inherited privilege; and

- Political consultants who advise their clients to use negative campaigning, as they are often more effective than efforts to remain positive.

But the vast amount of our research indicates that, the *extreme* level of *partisanship* and *political polarization,* we are currently experiencing in America is having a significantly negative impact on our country's ability to be a kindlier, and more humane place to call home.

Over the past few decades, *polarization* and *partisan conflict* has also led to, *inaction,* on major social, environmental, and global concerns. Ideologically rigid mentalities lower the probability of achieving the *compromise,* that should be at the *heart,* of legislative functioning.

An Approach to Counter the Impact

Yes. Our research indicates that it is true.

The *Influence of Partisan Politics* does indeed challenge our *capacity for sympathy,* and our *ability to honestly participate in the feelings, beliefs, and emotions* of other people.

But there is no need to feel hopeless. Our research also reflects that most Americans, do not want to see the kind of division that the current level of political polarization is creating. Most Americans, *across political spectrums,* want to build a shared, and more humane society.

Andrew Hanauer, President/CEO of the *One America Movement,* an organization founded by faith and community leaders, to address polarization in American society, shared the thoughts below — which may be used to help counter the impact, and possibly, *bridge the divide,* and prevent deeper polarization.

Take divisive media with a grain of salt.

Much of the division in our country is fed on a national level with news and social media headlines, leading the way. Regardless of the topic, the story is often presented as one group, against another.

Focus on local communities.

One of the best ways we can combat that dangerous tendency to lump groups in with extremists, is to remember, and honor the nuances of others. This is easier to do at the local level, where we can look people in the eyes, and have an honest conversation.

Honor our democracy.

The deep division we are stuck in has led many to support their party or politicians at all costs. As a result, we've seen a re-writing of the rules to fit any given narrative. We must hold politicians, and ourselves accountable, at all times, no matter who we think it benefits. To do otherwise, is to turn our backs on who we are, as a country.

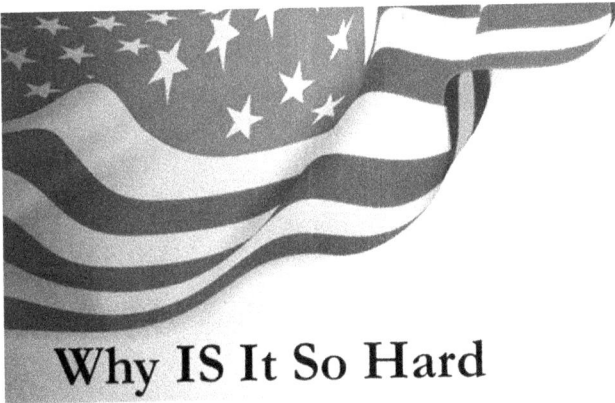

Why IS It So Hard

CHAPTER NINE
The Influence of Partisan Politics

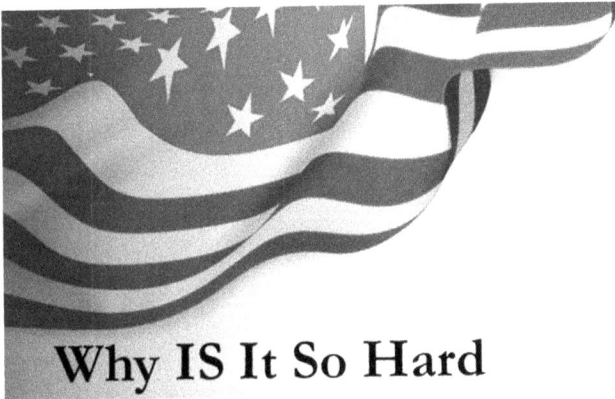

Why IS It So Hard

The Influence of Wealth and Power

"To understand the story of humanity is to bear witness to the story of its greatest paradox [which is]- power. This phenomenon creates the constraints in which we operate, yet is responsible for the structures that bind our society together. The exercise and accumulation of power is endemic to humanity. In the 20th century alone, this phenomenon has been responsible for over 200 million deaths through war and oppression and has concentrated over 50% of the world's wealth into the hands of just 1% of the world's population, meaning that billions of our global family, have been subjected to hunger, thirst, and disease. Power has also enabled social movements that have brought rights, freedoms and opportunity to many billions more."

—2014 article by Vikas Shah, Vikas Shah MBE DL is an entrepreneur, investor and philanthropist. He is also the CEO of the Swiscot Group

According to Schwab's 2021 Modern Wealth Survey, most Americans say that to be considered "wealthy" in the U.S. in 2021, you need to have a net worth of nearly $2 million and that wealth confers political power.

During our research into the impact of the *Influence of Wealth and Power* on an American's humanity, and an individual's desire to become a *people person*, we were intrigued by the perspective shared by Vikas Shah, CEO of the Swiscot Group, in the excerpt at the beginning of this Chapter. His implication that, *"to understand the story of humanity, is to bear witness to the story of its greatest paradox — [which is] power"*, led us to broaden the typical research on this topic, beyond just the discussion of the *growing inequality of wealth* and *power* in America.

As we ventured down this road of inquisitiveness, we began to take a deeper and deeper dive. In the process, we found ourselves searching for the answer to, perhaps the most important *question*, we should be asking about the influences of wealth and power. *What are the societal side effects of the paradox of the sometime humane and then often inhumane actions taken by those Americans who have obtained wealth and power?*

In the context of this *question*, when we refer to *paradox*, we are referring to what is defined as a *"social paradox"*. A *social paradox* is defined as *a pervasive, continuing dilemma between incompatible yet interdependent activities.*

The best example of a *social paradox* is *"Race has no physical basis, but the social paradox makes racism appeal to many people nonetheless"*. When we refer to *societal side effects*, we are suggesting *recognizable outcomes* due to the *actions* or *inactions* of those with wealth and political power, which are *unintended*, however constrains a society from practicing *humanitarianism* or an active belief in the value of human life.

But, before we discuss what we found there, we will first, remind most, and perhaps enlightened some, of the degree to which, the *inequality* in the distribution of wealth in our country has widened over the past few decades. Many may be surprised to realize the size, and the pace of the consolidation of *real power,* within our democracy. A consolidation, which has placed more wealth in the hands, of a smaller number of Americans.

Then, we will reveal what we discovered, regarding the *societal side-effects* of the *paradox* or *inconsistency* of the activities of America's most wealthy, and the barriers they place in the few avenues available, to most Americans, in their struggles to become more humane, and caring people.

Income Inequality in America Today

The following excerpt addresses the *rise of inequality in America,* and the *blindness,* that many of the wealthiest Americans have of its implications. We believe that this message appropriately frames the attitudes of many Americans, regarding the challenges associated with, the high level of income *inequality* that exist in our country today. The excerpt is taken from an article written by Dacher Keltner, a professor of psychology at the University of California, Berkeley and co-author of a 2010 research study, *The Rich Are Different: More Money, Less Empathy.* The article was published in the magazine, *Psychological Science.*

"We are living in a period of historically high inequality. Health problems and psychological problems are correlated with inequality and we have rising inequality. People in positions of [wealth and] power are not going to see [the inequality]. They're going to be blind to it and that has enormous implications for how, we educate leaders, why they may not see [what's] obvious [to everyone else], and why they may not even understand the suffering of the people below them."

The graph below clearly displays the degree to which, the *inequality* of the distribution of wealth in our country, has widened over the last fifty-five years.

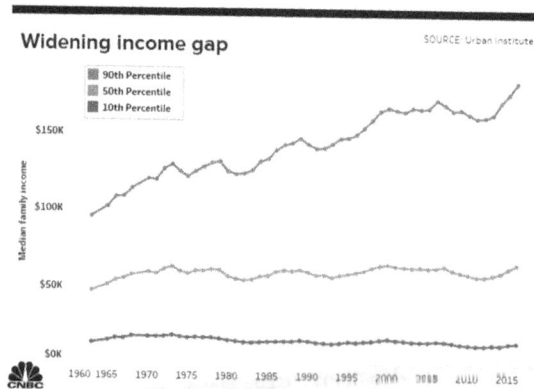

Widening income gap — SOURCE Urban Institute

The Reasons for Income Inequality and Why it Matters

According to information released by the Pew Research Center, in a January 2020 report:

"The rise in economic inequality in the U.S. is tied to several factors. These include, in no particular order, technological change, globalization, the decline of unions and the eroding value of the minimum wage. Whatever the causes, the uninterrupted increase in inequality since 1980 has caused concern among members of the public, researchers, policymakers and politicians.

One reason for the concern is that people in the lower rungs of the economic ladder may experience diminished economic opportunity and mobility in the face of rising inequality, a phenomenon referred to as The Great Gatsby Curve.

Others have highlighted inequality's negative impact on the political influence of the disadvantaged, on geographic segregation by income, and on economic growth itself. The matter may not be entirely settled, however, as an opposing viewpoint suggests that income inequality does not harm economic opportunity."

In the chart below, The Pew Research Center indicates that the share of American adults who live in middle-income households has decreased from 61% in 1971 to 51% in 2019.

The gaps in income between upper-income and middle- and lower-income households are rising, and the share held by middle-income households is falling

Median household income, in 2018 dollars, and share of U.S. aggregate household income, by income tier

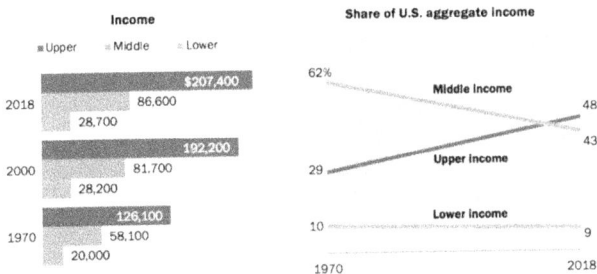

Income — ■ Upper ▪ Middle ▫ Lower

Income		Share of U.S. aggregate income
2018	$207,400 / 86,600 / 28,700	62% → Middle income → 48
2000	192,200 / 81,700 / 28,200	29 → Upper income → 43
1970	126,100 / 58,100 / 20,000	10 → Lower income → 9

1970 — 2018

Note: Households are assigned to income tiers based on their size-adjusted income. Incomes are scaled to reflect a three-person household. Revisions to the Current Population Survey affect the comparison of income data from 2014 onward. See Methodology for details.
Source: Pew Research Center analysis of the Current Population Survey, Annual Social and Economic Supplements (IPUMS).
"Most Americans Say There Is Too Much Economic Inequality in the U.S., but Fewer Than Half Call It a Top Priority"

PEW RESEARCH CENTER

Also, in their words, "*This downsizing has proceeded slowly but surely since 1971, with each decade thereafter typically ending with a smaller share of adults living in middle-income households than at the beginning of the decade.*" Through extensive research and analysis of comparative data, we found, without doubt, that the comparable income of most Americans, has been falling over the past four decades. As a result, the *inequality* of the distribution of wealth has widened.

Our research into the acceleration of the consolidation of *real power*, within our democracy, was also as extensive and insightful. In a February 8, 2019, article in the Washington Post, Christopher Ingraham, reported the following:

"*The concentration of U.S. wealth seems to have returned to levels last seen during the Roaring Twenties. That shift is eroding security from families in the lower and middle classes, who rely on their small stores of wealth to finance their retirement and to smooth over economic shocks like the loss of a job. And it's consolidating power in the hands of the nation's billionaires, who are increasingly using their riches to purchase political influence.*"

The 400 richest Americans now own more than the bottom 150 million

Share of American wealth owned by the 400 richest Americans

Share of American wealth owned by the bottom 60% (150 million in 2016)

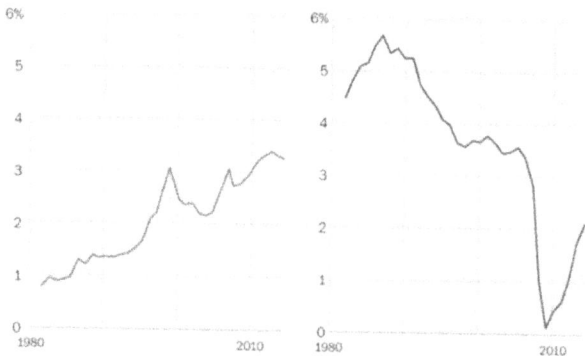

Source: Gabriel Zucman, World Inequality Database, The Washington Post

There is significant published research, which confirms that a vast amount of the aggregate income in America over the past few decades has been "gobbled up" by the top 10 percent of households. Here is one estimate provided by Carter C. Price and Kathryn A. Edwards of the RAND corporation in a working paper titled, *Trends in Income From 1975 to 2018*, of just how much wealth has been *consolidated* into the hands of fewer Americans.

"From 1975 to 2018, the difference between the aggregate taxable income for those below the 90th percentile, and the equitable growth, contrary to fact, does total, $47 trillion."

The Paradox of Wealth and Political Power

As you know, the power to effect *social change*, within America's political system is determined by who or what groups control the access points and methods of social influence.

The election of the U.S. President and Members of the U.S. Congress establishes the constitutional powers needed to maintain a functional federal government. From the selection and approval of the lifetime members of the U.S. Supreme Court to the appointment of Federal Judges, the executive and legislative branches of the U. S. Government are, without question, the primary access points of political power and social control and influence in America.

So, you might say that to maintain a justly *humanitarian society,* requires that we elect to these seats of political power, *individuals,* who are *capable* and *willing,* to champion humanitarian causes.

However, as we all know, in 21st century politics, a presidential or congressional candidate's ability to raise enormous sums of money and attract large partisan constituency, generally determine the success of elections and one's ability to reach these positions of power.

According to the Center for Responsive Politics, in October 2020, *"The total cost of the 2020 election will nearly reach an unprecedented $14 billion, making it the most expensive election in history and twice as expensive as the previous presidential election cycle."*

2020 Election to Crush Spending Records

OpenSecrets projects total federal spending in the 2020 election will near $14 billion, establishing itself as the most expensive election in U.S. history by a large margin.

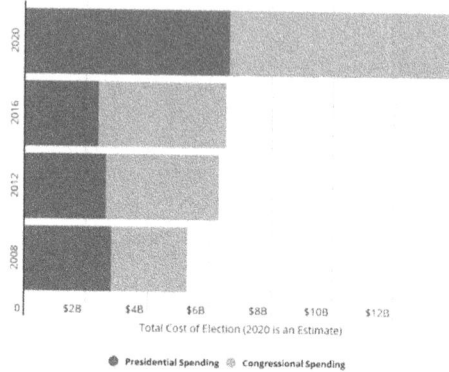

Total Cost of Election (2020 is an Estimate)

● Presidential Spending ⊛ Congressional Spending

Source: OpenSecrets.org

As we mentioned in Chapter One, in our research, we have come to believe that, in the purest sense, humanitarian cultures have *transformative forces*, which can lay the foundation for resolving issues, within the American society, that *wealth, political power,* selfishness, celebrity, threats, coercion, regulations, punishment or physical destruction have failed to do, since human existence.

We began our deeper research into this topic from this launching point. As we analyzed more and more data, we became convinced, that undeniably, one of the most important questions, we should be asking about the influences of *wealth* and *power* is not where it resides, but what are the *societal side effects* of the paradoxes of America's *wealthy* and *powerful,* which has written and continues to write *the story of humanity* within our country.

We concluded at the end of our research in this area, that providing *examples,* would be the best approach, for us to share a portion of what we discovered. We believe that, just a glimpse, into the most transparent *paradoxes,* associated with America's use of its *wealth* and *political power,* is quite revealing.

A couple of examples follow. Each example summarizes the type of *paradox* and the unintentional, but troublesome, *societal side-effects,* which have historically contributed, to the writing of America's *story of humanity.*

Example One

The Paradox: *"Access to quality, affordable health care is a <u>basic human right</u> that <u>every</u> American deserves."*

What Most Americans Desire and are Saying:

- According to the Pew Research Center 2017 survey, 60% of Americans say the government should be responsible for ensuring health care coverage for all Americans, compared with 38% who say this should not be the government's responsibility.

- In a 2020 Pew Research Center survey, 68% of voters say health care is very important to their vote.

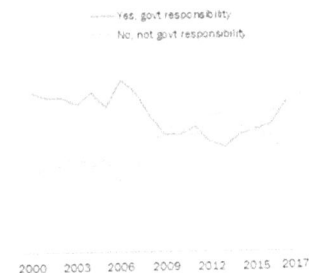

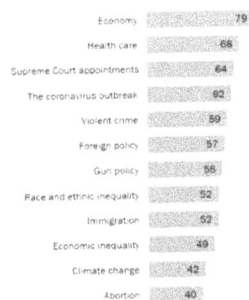

What the Wealthy and Powerful are Doing:

- In 2016, according to National Health Expenditures Accounts, nongovernment [public] philanthropic spending reached approximately $203 billion, or only about 10% of all health spending annually in the United States. This includes the Bill and Melinda Gates Foundation's Center of Vaccine Research and its commitment of $1.75 billion for pandemic relief.

- The Republican Party has been trying for a decade to repeal healthcare benefits for 31 million Americans, and as of August 2020, twelve Republican Governors are denying federally paid Medicaid expansion.

The Societal Side Effect: *According to the Congressional Budget Office, the number of American citizens who are uninsured in 2020 is around 31 million and According to U.S. News and World Report in an April 2021 article, The U.S. public health system currently ranks No. 22, among industrialized countries, falling seven spots on the list compared to 2020.*

Example Two

The Paradox: *"America's Social Justice System keeps its citizens safe with more criminal arrests, prosecutions, police and prisons."*

What Most Americans Desire and are Saying:

- Public attitudes about crime differ by Americans' partisan affiliation, race and ethnicity and other factors. However, a 2017 survey conducted for the ACLU's Campaign for Smart Justice indicated, *"Most Americans (67%) believe that building more prisons and jails does not reduce crime."*

- Both the FBI and BJS data show dramatic declines in U.S. violent and property crime rates since the early 1990s, when crime spiked across much of the nation.

- According to the Pew Research Center in a 2019 Report, *"Property crime in the U.S. is much more common than violent crime."*

- According to *Statista*, the U.S. leads world countries with the largest number of prisoners per 100,000 of the national population, as of July 2021

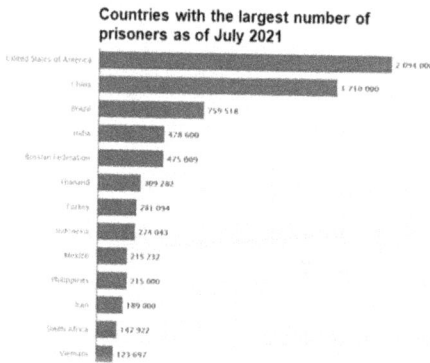

Countries with the largest number of prisoners as of July 2021

Theft is most common property crime, assault is most common violent crime

U.S. crime rates per 100,000 people, by offense type, in 2019

PEW RESEARCH CENTER

What the Wealthy and Powerful are Doing:

- Most conservative politicians focus reelections and raise major funds on themes of preventing violent crime and on "law and order".

- According to the Brennan Center for Justice, *"a handful of wealthy donors dominate electoral giving and spending in the United States, and social justice reform is not on the top of their list."*

Societal Side Effect: According to American Action Forum, *"The societal costs of incarceration include lost earnings, adverse health effects, and the damage to the families of the incarcerated. These costs are estimated at up to three times the direct costs, bringing the total burden of our criminal justice system to $1.2 trillion."*

The Impact of the Influence of *Wealth and Power*

We believe that the two examples we have provided, clearly reflects the significant influence the *wealthy* and *powerful* within America can have on our society's culture. As our research confirmed, because America's *story of humanity*, involves *social paradoxes*, created by political *decisions* and *actions* of the *wealthy* and *powerful*, most individuals striving to become *people persons* are emotionally and psychologically impacted by lingering social and cultural "wedge issues" — even when there is a majority consensus, nationally, on the most equitable, cost effective and humane solutions.

An Approach to Counter the Impact

As we mentioned earlier, the best approach to counter the impact of the *Influence of Wealth and Power,* would be to elect to seats of political power, *individuals,* who are *capable* and *willing,* to champion humanitarian causes.

Our research indicates that the rise of *income inequality* is one of the major impacts caused by the *social paradoxes* of the wealthy and powerful. Many Americans who lean conservative are concerned about a socialist uprising that could ruin American capitalism. While, to the contrary, most economist, who study the issue, *do not* believe that this would be the case.

We discovered that, many *constructive ideas* are being discussed and debated, in public and private circles around the country. Most of these ideas firmly embrace the kind of *thoughtful* and *bipartisan* approaches required to strengthen and grow *America's economy* — while at the same time, taking advantage of ways to strengthen *America's humanity.*

We believe that most informed Americans, are painfully aware that addressing an issue, as political as, *income inequality,* necessitates that, *we the people,* give our Congressional Representatives, the broad, public support they need, to *garner* and *sustain* the *"political will"* required, to get the job done.

CHAPTER TEN

The Influence of Wealth and Power

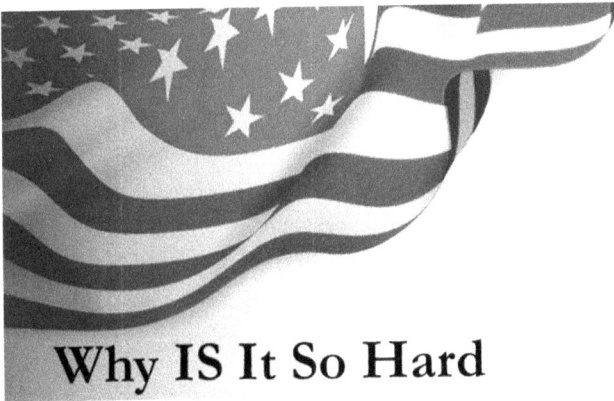

Why **IS** It So Hard

The Influence of Religious Hypocrisy

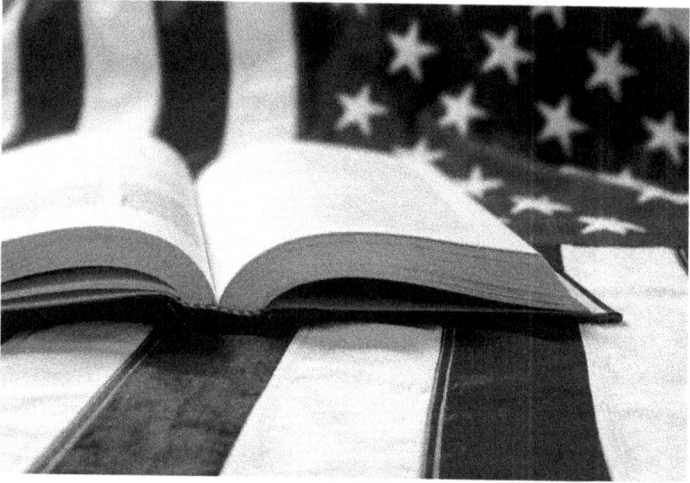

"We reject any teaching that encourages racial groups to view themselves as privileged oppressors or entitled victims of oppression," and *"We emphatically deny that lectures on social issues (or activism aimed at reshaping the wider culture) are as vital to the life and health of the church as the preaching of the gospel and the exposition of Scripture."*

— From **"For the Sake of Christ and His Church: The Statement on Social Justice and the Gospel", September 2018.**

In our characterization of a *people person*, we emphasize the need for such an individual to *"strive to bring out the best in oneself, as a human being and respecting the uniqueness and the humanity of others."* We also emphasized in Chapter One, our belief that, the word *humanity*, embraces what's most positive within us as *human beings* — including *kindness, compassion, honesty, tolerance towards differences, respect for others, integrity and thoughtfulness.*

According to Tom Gjelten, Religion and Belief Correspondent for National Public Radio news, in a story published on June 28, 2017, *"America's exceptional commitment to religious freedom stems from the diversity of its faith traditions. The rebellious attitudes prevalent in frontier settlements fostered the growth of evangelical movements. African slaves introduced Islam to America. The drive to abolish slavery was led largely by Christian preachers."* In hindsight, one must believe that the *exceptional commitment to religious freedom* and the *diversity of faith traditions,* of which Gjelten refers, encompassed a deep respect for humanity. All three of the accomplishments he highlighted, required some degree of *kindness, compassion, honesty, tolerance towards differences, respect for others, integrity and thoughtfulness.*

While the United States is a secular nation, meaning that by law, there is a formal separation between state and religious entities, our American society is saturated in strong principles of individual and religious freedom. Principles, which emphasize an individual's freedom to worship any religion and for the *law of the land* to not favor one religion over another. Though, most of us would agree, that along with being a *secular nation,* America often functions and organizes daily life, as a *religious nation.*

The United States census does not contain questions about one's religious affiliation. However, a 2014 Pew Research Center found that in America, *"Christianity is the largest religious affiliation at 70.6%. Non-Christian religions made up 5.9% of the population, of which 1.9% identified as Jewish, 0.9% identified as Muslim, 0.7% identified as Buddhist and 0.7% identified as Hindu."* In addition, in the survey, only *"22.8% identified as unaffiliated, which includes agnostics (4.0%) and atheists (3.1%)".*

In a July 2020 report, the Pew Research Center indicated that, *"Congress has always been overwhelmingly Christian, and roughly nine-in-ten representatives (88%) in the current Congress identify as Christian, and that Americans are divided on the extent to which the country's laws should reflect Bible teachings. Roughly half of U.S. adults say the Bible should influence U.S. laws either a great deal (23%) or some (26%), and more than a quarter (28%) say the Bible should prevail over the will of the people if the two are at odds. Half of Americans, meanwhile, say the Bible shouldn't influence U.S. laws much (19%) or at all (31%)".*

**The religious makeup
of the 116th Congress**

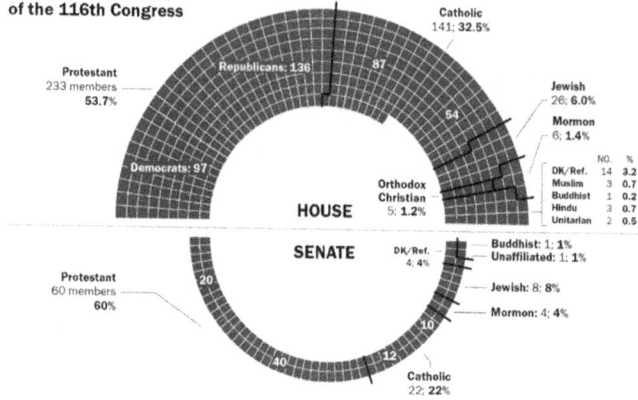

Catholic
141; **32.5%**

Protestant
233 members
53.7%

Republicans: 136

87

Jewish
26; **6.0%**

Mormon
6; **1.4%**

54

	NO.	%
DK/Ref.	14	3.2
Muslim	3	0.7
Buddhist	1	0.2
Hindu	3	0.7
Unitarian	2	0.5

Democrats: 97

Orthodox
Christian
5; **1.2%**

HOUSE

SENATE

DK/Ref.
4; 4%

Buddhist: 1; 1%
Unaffiliated: 1; 1%

Protestant
60 members
60%

20

Jewish: 8; 8%

Mormon: 4; 4%

10

40

12

Catholic
22; **22%**

Note: Figures may not add to 100% or to subtotals due to rounding.
Figures for Democrats include two independents who caucus with Democrats.
Source: Figures for Congress based on Pew Research Center analysis of data collected
by CQ Roll Call, reflecting members of Congress to be sworn in on Jan. 3, 2019.
"Faith on the Hill: The religious composition of the 116th Congress."

PEW RESEARCH CENTER

Half of Americans say Bible should influence U.S. laws
28% favor it over the will of the people

Bible should have _____ influence on U.S. laws

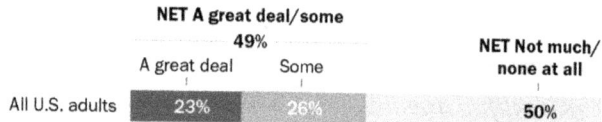

NET A great deal/some

49%

A great deal   Some

**NET Not much/
none at all**

All U.S. adults   **23%**   26%   **50%**

*If Bible and will of people conflict, which should have more
influence on U.S. laws?*

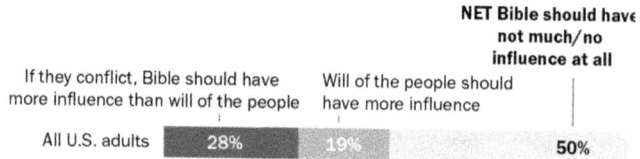

**NET Bible should have
not much/no
influence at all**

If they conflict, Bible should have
more influence than will of the people

Will of the people should
have more influence

All U.S. adults   **28%**   19%   **50%**

Note: Figures may not add to subtotals indicated due to rounding. Those who did
not answer are not shown.
Source: Survey conducted Feb. 4-15, 2020, among U.S. adults.
"White Evangelicals See Trump as Fighting for Their Beliefs, Though Many Have
Mixed Feelings About His Personal Conduct"

PEW RESEARCH CENTER

As we began our research into how the influence of religion affects most Americans, who are *"striving to bring out the best in oneself, as a human being and respecting the uniqueness and the humanity of others,* our initial focus was on religion's perceived role of guiding individual, and societal *religious morals* and *ethical behavior.* By ethical behavior, we are referring to moral principles based on well-founded standards of *right* and *wrong,* that prescribe what *we the people* should do, usually in terms of *rights, obligations, benefits to society, fairness,* or *specific virtues.*

Then, as we broaden our perspective and began to look deeper into the religion as espoused by the American church, meaning the body or organization of believers, and the role the church plays in shaping *societal behavior*, it quickly became obvious that the church's role is *misleadingly complex* and is a strategic mix of *faith* and *politics*.

Our research in this area reflects that throughout American history, the American church, and the religion, it endorses and preaches, has always compartmentalized *personal spirituality* and *social engagement*. Even though this *selective separation* of church and state should not be a surprise to any of us, the degree and magnitude by which this *compartmentalization* impacts, and influences the broader society and *wider culture* might not be as obvious.

We would consider all three of the actions *aimed at reshaping the wider American culture,* referred to by Tom Gjelten in his quote, as representative of a multitude of religiously influenced societal interactions, which have occurred since America's founding. They all have characteristics of being both *spiritual* and *social* engagements. However, our research revealed that maintaining such a humanitarian balance in major social interactions, within a diverse and rebellious American society, is a formidable challenge.

We purposely used the excerpt from a document titled, *"For the Sake of Christ and His Church: The Statement on Social Justice and the Gospel",* to open our discussion on this topic. We believe that the wording and intention of this statement is representative of how the *compartmentalization* of *personal spirituality* and *social engagement* can selfishly sacrifice the *good of society* for the *exposition of Scripture*. This is an obviously sincere, yet paradoxical practice, which not only complicates the sensitive societal interaction required to address *conflicting cultural* beliefs, but also makes *religion*, in general, appear to be *contradictory* and sometimes *hypocritical*.

In this light, we concluded our research into the *Influence of Religious Hypocrisy*, by taking a closer look into the wording of *"The Statement on Social Justice and the Gospel"*. It is a document signed by 4,700 pastors in 2018. The chart which follows, summarizes our approach and findings. During this exercise, we simply identified, what we perceive to be *contradictions*, that are exposed in this widely distributed, religious document. We believe that most Americans would view the document, as worded, as inconsistent with America's core democratic values and detrimental to societal unity and *humane social behavior*.

"We reject any teaching that encourages racial groups to view themselves as privileged oppressors or entitled victims of oppression."	▪ The act of teaching and freedom of expression are core values in the democratic process.
	▪ By referring specifically to *racial groups*, the message feeds into social divisiveness, and discourages civil discussion.
	▪ As worded, the statement appears to ignore the existence of privilege and social oppression, which exist in various forms, other than race, across vast spectrums of American life in the 21st Century.

"We emphatically deny that lectures on social issues (or activism aimed at reshaping the wider culture) are as vital to the life and health of the church as the preaching of the gospel and the exposition of Scripture."	▪ By emphatically denying and not listening to any *civil discussion* and *rationale* for *"reshaping the wider culture,"* the statement clearly suggests, that there is no interest in *compromise* – which is a primary quality of humane behavior. ▪ The prioritization of the *life and the health* of the *church*, higher that the *life and health* of the broader *society*, encourages *societal disunity*. ▪ These words send a strong message, that *social issues* and *activism aimed at reshaping the wider culture*, are contrary to biblical scripture - while, in Isaiah 1:17 the scripture reads : *"Learn to do good; seek justice, correct oppression; bring justice to the fatherless, and please the widow's cause"*.

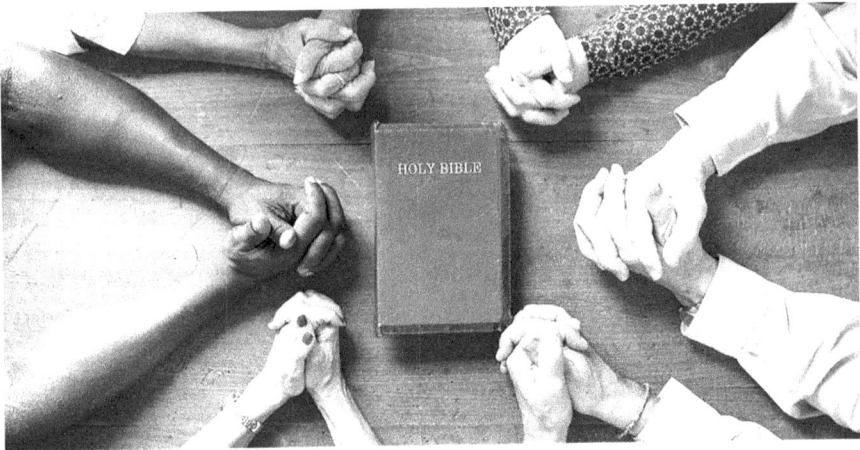

The Impact of the Influence of *Religious Hypocrisy*

— **Credit...Robb Davidson**

As we indicated earlier, our research found that religion's role in guiding both *religious morals* and *ethical behavior* within the American society is a *mixed bag*. Historically, its role has been *misleadingly complex* and is a strategic mix of *faith* and *politics*.

As we know, religion played a major role in the American Revolution by offering a moral sanction for opposition to the British, and that religion has historically played a role in conflict and warfare around the world. Despite public concerns about religious groups, and a loss of respect for clergy in general, many Americans still see religion generally having a positive role for American society.

Our research has found a multitude of work on *religion, human society* and *social justice* published over the past 100 years, which discusses the role of religion in social engagement. Most of the literature takes positions that are contrary to the *"Statement of Social Justice and the Gospel.*

One of the most profound and most original works published was written by sociologist Émile Durkheim in 1961, in his last major book titled, *"The Elementary Forms of Religious Life"*. Durkheim is recognized as the principal architect of the academic discipline of sociology. In his book, Durkheim argues:

"Religion is, in a sense, the celebration and even (self-) worship of human society. Religion provides social cohesion to help maintain social solidarity through shared rituals and beliefs, social control to enforce religious-based morals and norms to help maintain conformity and control in society, and it offers meaning and purpose to answer any existential questions. Religion is an expression of social cohesion."

As you will recall, in Chapter Four, we discussed the important role that *social cohesion* plays in consolidating plurality of citizenship, by reducing inequality, socioeconomic disparities and fractures in society.

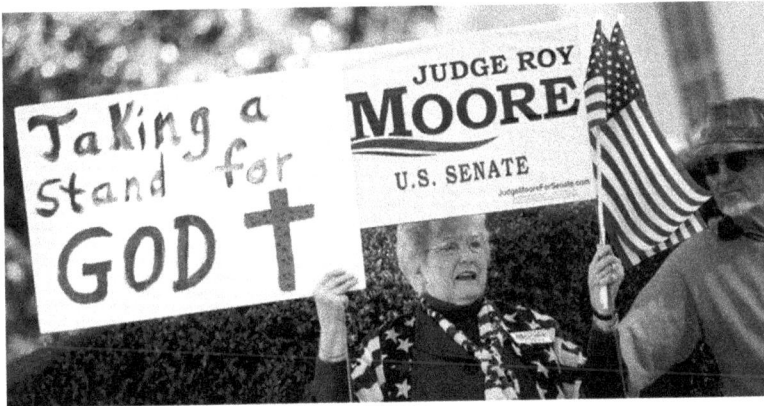

— **November 25, 2017. VOX.COM**

Furthermore, without going into specific details, our research identified many examples of the overarching, undeniable hypocrisy in conservative fundamentalist and evangelical circles in America over recent decades. It appears that their interpretation of morality shifts, back and forth, whenever the political price is right.

As confirmed by our research and that of many others, these types of *seesawing* religious practices only serve to complicate the sensitive societal interaction required to address *conflicting cultural* beliefs and make *religion* appear to be *contradictory* and sometimes *hypocritical.*

In a June 2015 study titled, *"Religion's Role in Political Socialization"*, Madison Dayton Daines and Quin Monson of Brigham Young University, indicated that *"religious and political socialization interacts to influence political attitudes and behaviors".*

We believe that our research confirms that the *religious power* associated with influencing both *social* and *political behaviors* in America, can have a significant impact on an individual who is honestly striving to become a *people person.*

One of the most insightful perspectives on *religious power* identified during our research was presented by Dr. Patricia Mische, the Lloyd Professor of Peace Studies and World Law at Antioch College, in an article published in 2017, in the Journal of Religion, Conflict, and Peace. The article is titled, *The Significance of Religions for Social Justice and a Culture of Peace.* In the article, Dr. Mische states:

"One reason that religions may have played a powerful role in history is that they often carry the archetypes, symbols, stories, and worldviews through which people shape their identity, designate their deepest questions of meaning, deal with problems of injustice and suffering, and develop codes of morality and conduct to meet the requirements of community life. Because they function at often deep and unconscious levels, people are often unaware of the affect of religious symbols, archetypes and identity systems on their values, choices and behaviors. Nevertheless, people are often prepared to die in order to defend or uphold these symbols, meanings, and identity systems."

An Approach to Counter the Impact

Most of the impacts of the *Influence of Religious Hypocrisy* that are detrimental to *societal unity* and *humane social behavior,* are linked to the lack of religious advocacy to improve humanitarian conditions in *secular society.*

Our research found that one practical approach to counter the lack of constructive *religious influence* in addressing multicultural, and bipartisan social issues, *such as social justice, affordable healthcare, income inequality and sensible gun control,* is to personally become an advocate, for these concerns, within your religious affiliations.

Here are the four steps that one U.S. based religious organization, that is committed to addressing social concerns within the American society, recommends to its members, on how to address, and personally take own the challenge. The four steps are:

- *Support the vocation of members in their daily callings and work.*
- *Encourage learning and moral discernment.*
- *Develop and endorse social teaching and policy.*
- *Witness for social justice as individual Christians, and as organized faith communities.*

We have found that the best way to stay encouraged as an advocate in this area is to keep in mind a quote by the English writer, poet, and activist, Walter Savage Landor. Landor once said, *"There is nothing on earth divine, except humanity".*

CONCLUSION

As we mentioned in the Introduction, from the beginning of this project, the goal was to not try to persuade anyone that one set of thoughts, conclusions and beliefs are the only valid perspectives on this significant and thought-provoking topic. We simply sought to set forth a unique presentation of our extensive research, a documented and substantiated analysis, and the most relevant literary work of others on the topic, to set forth an *intelligent*, candid, and contemporary discussion.

As expressed by Adam Grant, an organizational psychologist at the Wharton School of the University of Pennsylvania, in his bestselling book titled, *Think Again: The Power of Knowing What You Don't Know:*

"Intelligence is usually seen as the ability to think and learn, but in a rapidly changing world, there's another set of cognitive skills that might matter more: the ability to rethink and unlearn. In our daily lives, too many of us favor the comfort of conviction over the discomfort of doubt. We listen to opinions that make us feel good, instead of ideas that make us think hard."

We believe that *Why Is It So Hard*, presents thoughtful *ideas* and potential solutions, regarding the lack of *humanity* and *kindness* within the American society today, which are openly dividing the country and summoning all of us, to *think hard* and maybe *think again*, about long held *beliefs, opinions* and *preferences* that are contributing to national disunity and distrust.

It is our hope that the common use of the metaphor, *People Person* and the positive proliferation of a *humanitarian vision* for the United States, will ignite insightful, intelligent and transformative conversations within civic-minded communities throughout the country. We believe that open-minded and purposeful discussions among, *we the people*, concerning the *four fundamental aspects* of American life, as set forth in the ten chapters of this book, can provide the momentum needed to move beyond the status quo.

In this regard, we conclude the following, based on the extensive research, objective analysis and the thoughts of scholars and subject matter experts presented within the pages of this book.

- The *search for societal unity within America* is more than a worthy cause. It is a national imperative — if we wish to extend the greatest and longest existing experiment in democracy the world has ever seen.

- The *role and power of humanity within daily life* must be fully understood, embraced and embedded within the *rules of societal interaction* at all crossroads of American society. This single action can significantly strengthen America's capacity to address the social, cultural, environmental and economic challenges currently being faced by all developed nations around the globe.

- *America's struggle with diversity and its past* is a historic reality. Moving beyond the *status quo*, and to competitively move into the 21st century, will require a reliable majority of Americans, to create a path short of another civil war, to help a plurality of Americans to understand, and buy into the value of accepting, teaching and learning from all of America's rich history. This action, along with the required changes in policies, would remove the burdens of the past that has seeded partisan politics and marginalized our country's full potential for centuries.

- The *invasiveness of societal influences* is omnipresent, *strategic*, and knowingly presents unavoidable psychological barriers, that prevent thoughtful Americans from becoming *people persons*. We must manage these influences to an acceptable level for the public good, and minimize the destructive forces of mass misinformation, polarization and selfishness.

If you have walked away, after reading this book, with similar conclusions, please share the book and your thoughts within your community. It just might ignite discussions that could lead to creating a nation of *people persons*.

ABOUT THE AUTHORS

Charlotte D. Grant-Cobb, PhD

Charlotte is a gifted author, change management coach, professional mentor and author. She is an International Coaching Federation (ICF) Certified Coach.

Charlotte's extensive resume includes over 30 years of professional accomplishment. She has held senior leadership positions within Fortune 100 corporations, small business enterprises as well as in Federal and State government.

Charlotte earned her Bachelor of Science degree in Management and a Master of Business Administration degree from *Arizona State University*. She has also earned a professional Doctor of Philosophy in Nutrition Counseling degree from *LaSalle University*.

Charlotte uses her gifts to help her clients gain new awareness, create new habits, forge new pathways and embrace new experiences.

Ervin (Earl) Cobb

Earl is an accomplished corporate executive, leadership development coach, lecturer, and author. He is currently the CEO & Managing Partner of Richer Life, LLC.

Earl has held senior technical and leadership positions within Fortune 100, Mid-market and Venture companies including *Honeywell, Inc.*, *Motorola, Inc.*, *The Reynolds and Reynolds Company* and *Wells Fargo Bank*. He is the former President, COO and CEO of the high-tech start-up, *MedContrax, Inc.*

Earl earned a Bachelor of Science degree in Electrical Engineering, with honors, from *Tennessee State University*. He graduated from *Arizona State University* with a Master of Science degree in Engineering.

Earl is a former Adjunct Professor of Management at the Keller Graduate School of Management of *DeVry University*. He has completed graduate studies at *Stanford University's Graduate School of Business, the Sloan School of Management at MIT* and the *Center for Creative Leadership*.

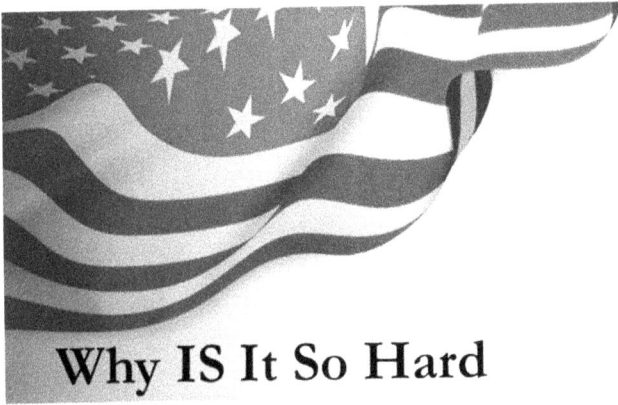

Why **IS** It So Hard

REFERENCES

INTRODUCTION

1. George, Janel. (January 12, 2021), *A Lesson on Critical Race Theory*: American Bar Association

2. Gregorian Dareh. (June 15, 2021), *"21 House Republicans Are Only Votes Against Bill To Honor Jan. 6 First Responders"*:NBC News.

CHAPTER ONE

3. Becker1999. (April 2020), COVID-19 *Anti-Lockdown Protests in the United States* : Grove City, OH.

4. Beckett, Lois. (April 2020), *Armed Protesters Demonstrate Against Covid-19 Lockdown at Michigan Capitol*: The Guardian New & Media Limited.

5. Bur, Jessie Bur. (September 8, 2020), *Trump Moves To End 'Un-American' Diversity Training For Feds*. Federaltimes.com

6. Censky, Abricail. (May 14, 2020), *Heavily Armed Protesters Gather Again At Michigan Capitol To Decry Stay-At-Home Order*: NPR

7. Center for Responsive Politics. *Influence & Lobbying*. (2021): opensecrets.org

8. Clark, Simon. (July 1, 2020), *How White Supremacy Returned to Mainstream Politics*: Center for American Progress.

9. Cobb, Jelani. (May 27, 2021), *The Death of George Floyd, in Context*: The New Yorker.

10. Corum, Samuel. (August 11, 2017), *Neo Nazis, Alt-Right, and White Supremacists march through the University of Virginia Campus with torches in Charlottesville, Va., USA*: Anadolu Agency: Getty Images.

11. Chhatwani, Anju. (August 16, 2014), *Importance of humanity: The most important religion is humanity*: Gulf News

12. Chiu , Ringo.(January 6, 2021), *Supporters of US President Donald Trump protest in Los Angeles*, Getty Images.

13. Cribb, T. Kenneth, Jr.; Brake, Richard; Scott, Gary Scott; Dautrich, Ken; Jeffery, Terrence and Ford, Patrick. (December 2009). *"The Shaping of the American Mind: The Diverging Influences of the College Degree & Civic Learning on American Beliefs"*: Intercollegiate Studies Institute.

14. Daniller, Andrew. (March 18, 2021), *Majorities of Americans See at Least Some Discrimination Against Black, Hispanic And Asian People in the U.S.*: Pew Research Center.

15. Fritze, John, (July 5, 2021), *Steady Term of the Supreme Court Ends with Politically Fraught Cases that Reveal Divisions*: USA TODAY.

16. Fox, Alison. (May 25, 2021), *FAA Says Airlines Have Reported about 2,500 Incidents of Unruly Passengers* : Travel + Leisure Co.

17. Glaser, James M., Berry, Jeffrey M. and Schildkraut, Deborah J.(January 20, 2020), *Education Makes People More Likely to Support Political Compromise…Except for Conservatives*: American Politics and Policy.

18. Haslam, Bill and Meacham, Jon. *Want Unity For Real? Then America Needs to Get Back to Facts*, (February 8, 2021):TIME Magazine

19. Highsmith, Carol M. Image from the Library of Congress, *Thomas Jefferson Building, the oldest structure in the Library of Congress complex*. (digital file no. LC-DIG-highsm-03196).

20. Horowitz Menasce, Juliana, Igielnik , Ruth and Kochhar, Rakesh. (January 9, 2020), *Most Americans Say There is too much Economic Inequality in the U.S., But Fewer than Half call it a Top Priority*: Pew Research Center.

21. J. E. Barbour. (1839), *The Jim Crow Song Book*: United States: New York, Ithaca: National Museum of American History.

22. Josephs, Leslie. (January 6, 2021), *Trump Supporters Protest At Statehouses Across The U.S. As Capitol Hill Demonstrations Turn Violent*: CNBC

23. Josephs, Leslie.(June 22, 2021), *It's Out of Control. Airlines, Flight Attendants Want Stiffer Penalties for Unruly Passengers*: CNBC.

24. Karimi, Karimi. (May 10, 2021), *What Critical Race Theory Is -- And Isn't* : CNN.

25. Kroeber, A. L. and C. Kluckhohn, (1952). *Culture: A Critical Review of Concepts and Definitions*. Peabody Museum, Cambridge, Massachusetts, United States.

26. Nawaz, Amna and Khanovements. (Oct 28, 2020), *How This Year's Antiracism Protests Differ from Past Social Justice Movements*: PBS News Hour

27. Leakey, Richard. (1996), *The Origin of Humankind*. New York: Basic Books.

28. Lipka, Michael.(April 13, 2020), *Half of Americans say Bible Should Influence U.S. Laws, Including 28% who favor it over the will of the people*: Pew Research Center.

29. Lumen Learning. Introduction to Psychology (2018),Societal Influence: State University of New York OER Services

30. McLeod, S. A. (2015), *Freud and the Unconscious Mind*: Simply Psychology

31. NCCS.net. *Unity: A Principle That Could Save America*, (June 2020): National Center for Constitutional Studies.

32. Patinkin, Jason. (May 31, 2020), *US Protests Could Bring Coronavirus Surge* : VOA News

33. Perrin, Andrew. (October 15, 2020), *23% of Users In U.S. Say Social Media Led Them to Change Views on an Issue; Some Cite Black Lives Matter*: Pew Research Center

34. Quintano, Anthony. (June 7, 2020), Black Lives Matter protest, Times Square, New York City: flicker (Photograph)

35. Rainie, Lee; Keeter, Scott and Perrin, Andrew, (July 22, 2019), *Trust and Distrust in America*: Pew Research Center.

36. Rasmussen, Scott. (Aug 24, 2020), *Is America too polarized? What more than 90% of Americans really want their leaders to do.*: Deseret News Publishing Company. Research Topics. *Less-Educated Americans More Inclined to see Some Truth in Conspiracy Theory that COVID-19 was Planned*, (June 4, 2020),Pew Research Center.

37. Ross, Breana and Montoya, Melissa, (May 26, 2021), *Critical Race Theory: What It Actually Means*: WINK Digital Media.

38. Rothwell, Jonathan and Makridis, Christos. (September 17, 2020), *Politics is Wrecking America's Pandemic Response:* The Brookings Institution

39. Schaeffer, Katherine. (March 24, 2021), Despite Wide Partisan Gaps in Views of Many Aspects of the Pandemic, Some Common Ground Exists: Pew Research Center

40. Schaub, Jean-Frédéric. (January 2019), *"Race Is about Politics: Lessons from History:"* Princeton University Press,

41. Shapiro, Sarah and Brown, Catherine, (February 21, 2018) *The State of Civics Education*: The Center for American Progress.

42. Simba, Malik. (2010)*Black Marxism and American Constitutionalism: An Interpretive History from Colonial Background to the Great Depression*: Kendall Hunt Publishing.

43. Tram, Michael. (April 5, 2021), *"EXPLAINER: Was officer's knee on Floyd's neck authorized?"*: AP News.

44. USAHello.org, (June 11, 2021), *Diversity in the United States of America*: USAHello.

45. U.S. History Primary Source Timeline. *The Post War United States, 1945-1968*: loc.gov: U.S. Library of Congress.

46. U.S. History Primary Source Timeline. *Great Depression and World War II, 1929-1945*: loc.gov: U.S. Library of Congress.

47. U.S. History Primary Source Timeline. *Progressive Era to New Era, 1900-1929*: loc.gov: U.S. Library of Congress.

CHAPTER TWO

48. Fichera, Angelo. (April 23, 2021), *Posts Mislead on Words of Alternate Juror in Chauvin Trial*:Factcheck.org.

49. Gambardello, Joseph A. (November 20, 2020), *Bogus Report Claims Philly Mob Boss Stuffed Ballot Boxes:* Factcheck.org.

50. Gambardello, Joseph A. (March 10, 2021),*Capital Protestors Were Armed With Variety of Weapons*Factcheck.org.

51. Gore, D'Angelo Gore. (June 10, 2021), *Facebook Post Misleads on Bipartisan Capitol Attack Report and Interview.*Factcheck.org

52. Kahneman, Daniel. (2011) *Thinking, Fast and Slow.* Farrar, Straus and Giroux.

53. Spencer, Saranac Hale. (April 1, 2021), *Unfounded Claims About Colorado Gunman:*Factcheck.org

CHAPTER THREE

54. Crocker, Jennifer, Canevello, Amy and Brown, Ashley A. (January 2017), *Social Motivation: Costs and Benefits of Selfishness and Otherishness:* Annual Review of Psychology.

55. Henricks, Thomas Henricks. (June 24, 2021), *Does American Society Encourage Selfishness? : Our social institutions support a preoccupation with self:* Psychology Today.

56. Hutson, Matthew. (June 9, 2016), *We Tend To Be Cooperative—Unless We Think Too Much:* Nautilus Magazine.

57. Mazza, Ed. (July 23, 2021), *GOP Governor Says It's Time To Blame The Unvaccinated For Pandemic Surge* : HuffPost.

58. McCullough, Marie McCullough. (April 27, 2021), *COVID-19 Vaccine Hesitancy: Understandable and Irrational:* The Philadelphia Inquirer.

59. Ugochukw, Nnaemeka.(July 23, 2019), *How Society Got Broken: The Age of Selfishness and Narcissism* :Eco Warrior Princess.

CHAPTER FOUR

60. Andrew DeMello. (July 17, 2021), *GOP Governor's Vaccination Tour Reveals Depths of Distrust.* AP News.

61. Cara Murez. (April 29, 2021), Poll Reveals Who's Most Vaccine-Hesitant in America and Why: HealthDay Reporter.

62. Eggers, William D. Eggers, Chew, Bruce Chew, Knight, Joshua and Krawiec, RJ. (March 2021), Rebuilding trust in government: Four signals that can help improve citizen trust and engagement: Deloitte Global.

63. Ehrlich, Thomas. (2000), Civic Responsibility and Higher Education: Rowman & Littlefield Publishers.

64. George, Robert P. (2015), "The Thriving Society: On The Social Conditions of Human Flourishing": The Witherspoon Institute.

65. Kenton, Will and Perez, Yarilet. (July 24, 2021), Social Capital: Investopedia

66. Richardson, Daniel. (July 1, 2021), Exploring Barriers to COVID-19 Vaccination and Reasons for Vaccine Hesitancy. The HERO Registry.

67. Robson, David. (July 22, 2021), Why Some People Don't Want a Covid-19 Vaccine: BBC.

CHAPTER FIVE

68. Campbell, David Edward. (March 24, 2006),*Civic Engagement and Education: An Empirical Test of the Sorting Model*: Midwest Political Science Association.

69. De-Wit, Lee, Van Der Linden, Sander and Brick, Cameron (July 2, 2019), What Are the Solutions to Political Polarization?: Social psychology reveals what creates conflict among groups and how they can come together.: Greater Good Magazine.

70. Curry, James M. and Lee, Frances E. (Sep 22, 2020), *"The Limits of Party: Congress and Lawmaking in a Polarized Era"*: University of Chicago Press.

71. Political polarization update. (April 26, 2016), *A Wider Ideological Gap Between More and Less Educated Adults*: Pew Research Center.

72. Runciman, David. (October 16, 2016), *How the Education Gap is Tearing Politics Apart:* Guardian.

CHAPTER SIX

73. Southwell, Brian; Sheble, Laura, and Thorson, Emily. (January 24, 2018) *Misinformation and Mass Audiences*: University of Texas Press.

CHAPTER SEVEN

74. Allington, Daniel. *"Conspiracy Theories, Radicalization and Digital Media"*: GNET.

75. Brotherton, Rob. (January 3, 2017), Suspicious Minds: *Why We Believe Conspiracy Theories*: Bloomsbury Sigma.

76. Douglas, Karen M., Uscinski, , Joseph E., Sutton, Robbie M., Cichocka, Aleksandra, Nefes, Turkay, Chee Ang, Siang Chee, Deravi, Farzin. (March 20, 2019), *Understanding Conspiracy Theories:* John Wiley & Sons, Inc.

77. Fitz, Nicholas Fitz. (March 31, 2015), *Economic Inequality: It's Far Worse Than You Think: The Great Divide Between Our Beliefs, Our Ideals, and Reality:* Scientific American.

78. Friedman, Richard A. (July 24, 2020), *Why Humans Are Vulnerable to Conspiracy Theories*: The American Psychiatric Association.

79. Schaeffer, Katherine. (July 24, 2020), *A Look at the Americans who Believe There is Some Truth to the Conspiracy Theory that COVID-19 Was Planned:* Pew Research Center.

80. Staff Study. (March 2021), *Understanding QAnon's Connection to American Politics, Religion, and Media Consumption:* PRRI-IFYC.

81. Todd, Chuck, Murry, Mark and Dann Carrie (May 27, 2021), *Study Finds Nearly One-In-Five Americans Believe Qanon Conspiracy Theories:* NBC News/Meet The Press.

82. van Prooijen, Jan-Willem, Douglas, Karen M. (June 29, 2017), *Conspiracy Theories as Part of History: The Role of Societal Crisis Situations.* Sage Journals.

CHAPTER EIGHT

83. Desilver, Drew. (February 11, 2021), *U.S. Senate has Fewest Split Delegations Since Direct Elections Began:* Pew Research Center.

84. Edsall, Thomas B.(January 28, 2015), *How Did Politics Get So Personal?:* New York Times.

85. Hanauer, Andrew (April 2, 2021), Political polarization is now toxic in America. Here's how to stop it: USA Today.

86. Iyengar, Shanto and Westwood, Sean J. (December 16, 2014), *Fear and Loathing across Party Lines: New Evidence on Group Polarization.* American Journal of Political Science.

87. Staff Report. (June 12, 2014), *How Increasing Ideological Uniformity and Partisan Antipathy Affect Politics, Compromise and Everyday Life:* Pew Research Center.

CHAPTER NINE

88. Benenson Strategy Group. (November 16, 2017), *91 percent of Americans support criminal justice reform, ACLU polling finds.* American Civil Liberties Union.

89. Carter C. Price, Carter C. and Edwards, Kathryn. (2020), *Trends in Income From 1975 to 2018*: RAND Corporation.

90. Gramlich, John. (November 20, 2020), *What the data says (and doesn't say) about crime in the United States:* Pew Research Center .

91. Grewal, Daisy. (April 10, 2012), *How Wealth Reduces Compassion: As riches grow, empathy for others seems to decline.* Scientific American.

92. Horowitz, Juliana Menasce, Ruth Igielnik and Kochhar, Rakesh. (January 9, 2020), *Most Americans Say There Is Too Much Economic Inequality In The U.S., But Fewer Than Half Call It A Top Priority:* Pew Research Center.

93. Ingraham, Christopher. (February 8, 2019), *"Wealth concentration returning to 'levels last seen during the Roaring Twenties,' according to new research"*: Washington Post.

94. Kiley, Jocelyn, (OCTOBER 3, 2018), *Most continue to say ensuring health care coverage is government's responsibility.* Pew Research Center.

95. McKernan, Signe-Mary, Ratcliffe, Caroline Ratcliffe, Steuerle, C. Eugene, Quakenbush, Caleb, and Kalish, Emma. (February 2015): *Nine Charts about Wealth Inequality in America (Updated):* Urban Institute.

96. OpenSecrets.org (October 28, 2020), *2020 election to cost $14 billion, blowing away spending records*: Center for Responsive Politics.

97. Shah, Vikas. (February 4, 2021), *Thought Economics: Conversations with the Remarkable People Shaping Our Century*: Michael O'Mara.

98. Statista Research Department. (June 2, 2021), *Incarceration rates in selected countries 2021*: Statista.

99. Szalavit, Maia. (November 24, 2010), *The Rich Are Different: More Money, Less Empathy*: TIME.

CHAPTER TEN

100. Daines, Madison Dayton and Monson, Quin. (June 2015), *Religion's Role in Political Socialization*: Counseling Today. American Counseling Association.

101. Durkheim, Émile. (1961). The elementary forms of the religious life. New York: Collier Books.

102. Fahmy, Dalia. (July 16, 2020), *8 Facts About Religion and Government in the United States*: Pew Research Center.

103. Gjelten, Tom. (June 28, 2017), *To Understand How Religion Shapes America, Look To Its Early Days*: National Public Radio News.

104. Grant-Adam. (2021), *Think Again: The Power of Knowing What You Don't Know*: Viking

105. MacArthur, John MacArthur. (September 2018), *For the Sake of Christ and His Church: The Statement on Social Justice and the Gospel*: The Relevant Magazine.

106. Mische, Patricia.(2017), *The Significance of Religions for Social Justice and a Culture of Peace*: Journal of Religion, Conflict, and Peace.

107. Religious Landscape Study.(2014*), Exploring Religious Groups in the U.S. by Tradition, Family and Denomination*: Pew Research Center.

108. Mische, Patricia.(2017), *The Significance of Religions for Social Justice and a Culture of Peace*: Journal of Religion, Conflict, and Peace.

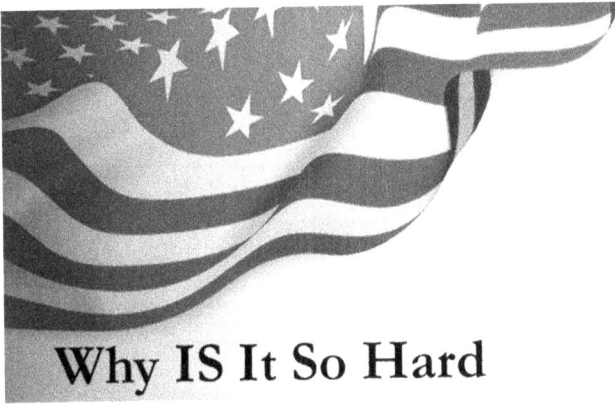

THOUGHTS TO PONDER AND SHARE

As we have mentioned, from the beginning of this literary project, the goal was to not try to persuade anyone that one set of *thoughts, conclusions* and *beliefs* are the only valid perspectives on this significant and thought-provoking topic.

To this point, we have included the following pages for you to use to note and *ponder* your own thoughts, conclusions and perspectives, based on what you are currently reading or have read thus far, in this book.

Why is this important? Because chances are, the *thoughts, conclusions* and *beliefs* you move forward with, after an attentive read of *Why Is It So Hard* will most likely, be the *thoughts, conclusions* and *beliefs* you will *live with* and *act upon* for the rest of your life — as they pertain to this collectively critical topic.

By *ponder*, in this context, we are referring to you taking the time to *deeply think* about the *facts, data, inferences,* and *perspectives,* as well as the impartial compilation of the most relevant, *historic* and *contemporary,* thoughts of scholars, community activists, and media professionals, that are carefully woven, throughout the book's candid, and unbiased discussions.

We believe that it would be beneficial to thoughtfully consider, at a minimum, the following:

- Now that I have a better understanding of my humanity [i.e., *kindness, compassion, honesty, courage, tolerance towards differences, empathy, respect, integrity, thoughtfulness, etc.*] and the significant role it plays, or could play, in America and in

American life, what can I do or changes should I make for me to live a more humane life?

- By being aware that *most of the opinions, beliefs and perspectives that arise in my conscious experience got there, without me knowing how or when*, what should I do to become more skeptical of my own opinions, beliefs and perspectives and uncover the potential *errors* in my impressions, intuitions and decisions?

- Through my understanding that the American society is not a gathering of people, but the complex pattern of *rules of interaction* and what actually *resides in the minds* of individual Americans, what should I do to modify my perceptions of, and more properly respond to, the actions of others?

- Due to the invasiveness of societal influences in my daily life, what should I do to be able to effectively "connect the dots", become a knowledgeable skeptic of misinformation, and maintain a healthier perspective of my future?

Regardless of your conclusions and perspectives, sharing and broadly discussing your thoughts and beliefs within your personal and professional networks, regarding the thirteen primary topics highlighted on the following pages, will aid in providing you more clarity, informing others of the importance of considering the *causes and effects* and generating more *food for thought*.

Our research into the many, interrelated aspects of this topic, has convinced us, that open-minded conversations across the country and the potential changes in *people* and *policy*, can help eliminate many of the barriers that are currently impacting those Americans, striving to become *people persons*.

However, as we all know, a kinder and more humane society, starts with more thoughtful, civically involved, and kinder people.

Thoughts to Ponder and Share

The Search for Social Unity Within America

Thoughts to Ponder and Share

The Role of Humanity Within Daily Life

Thoughts to Ponder and Share
America's Struggle With Diversity and Its Past

Thoughts to Ponder and Share

The Invasiveness of Societal Influences

Thoughts to Ponder and Share
The Influence of The Human Mind

Thoughts to Ponder and Share
The Influence of Selfishness

Thoughts to Ponder and Share
The Influence of Apathy and Indifference

The Influence of The Less Educated

Thoughts to Ponder and Share

The Influence of Social Media and Mass Misinformation

_____

_____

_____

_____

_____

_____

_____

_____

_____

_____

_____

_____

_____

_____

_____

Thoughts to Ponder and Share

The Influence of Conspiracy Theories

Thoughts to Ponder and Share
The Influence of Partisan Politics

_____

_____

_____

_____

_____

_____

_____

_____

_____

_____

_____

_____

_____

_____

_____

_____

Thoughts to Ponder and Share
The Influence of Wealth and Power

Thoughts to Ponder and Share
The Influence of Religious Hypocrisy

_____

_____

_____

_____

_____

_____

_____

_____

_____

_____

_____

_____

_____

_____

_____

_____

_____

OTHER BOOKS BY

Ervin (Earl) Cobb and Charlotte D. Grant-Cobb, PhD

Living a More Thoughtful Life
Thinkable Thoughts and Relevant Reflections

Situations and Leadership
Short Stories and Lifelong Lessons

Leadership Front and Center
A Decade of Thought and Tutelage

The SMART Leader and the Skinny Principles
How to Win and Lead within Any Organization

Driving Ultimate Project Performance
Transforming from Project Manager to Project Leader

**The Official Leadership Checklist and Diary
for Project Management Professionals**

The Leadership Advantage
Do More. Lead More. Earn More.

God's Goodness & Our Mindfulness
Responding versus Reacting to Life Changing Circumstances

Focused Leadership
What You Can Do Today To Become a More Effective Leader

Transition
Solace and Comfort for the Broken Hearted

Pillow Talk Consciousness
Intimate Reflections on America's 100 Most Interesting
Thoughts and Suspicions

Navigating the Life Enrichment Model™

Living a Richer Life
Getting the Most out of Life's Gifts and Circumstances

Until I Change
Affirmations for Mastering Personal Change

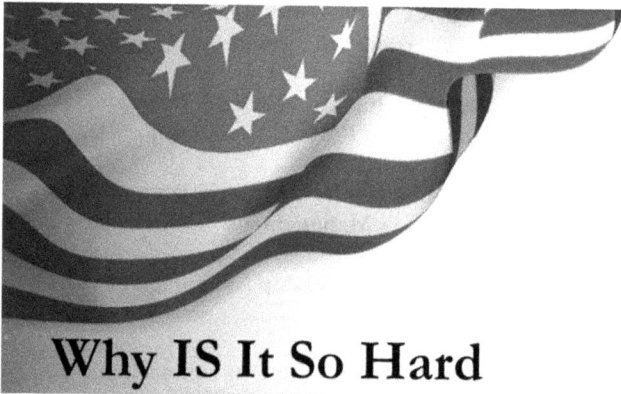

Why IS It So Hard

www.ingramcontent.com/pod-product-compliance
Lightning Source LLC
Chambersburg PA
CBHW071024280326
41935CB00011B/1473